fabric leftovers

fabric
leftovers

Simple, adaptable ways
to use up scraps

D'Arcy-Jean Milne

For Duncan: Love is enough

FABRIC LEFTOVERS
By D'Arcy-Jean Milne

First published in North America
by C&T Publishing Inc.,
PO Box 1456, Lafayette, CA 94549

Copyright © Octopus Publishing Group Ltd 2006
Text copyright © D'Arcy-Jean Milne 2006

ISBN 978-1-57120-384-7

A CIP record of this book is available from the British Library

Set in ITC Century Light

Printed and bound in China by Toppan Printing Company Ltd

Senior Executive Editor: Anna Sanderson
Executive Art Editor: Rhonda Summerbell
Editor: Alison Bolus
Photography: Roger Dixon
Design: Vivienne Brar
Production: Faizah Malik

Contents

Introduction

What do you need to know about me? I think it's enough to say that I love fabric: shopping for it, playing with it, cutting it up and making things, and tearing them apart and starting again. I quilt, I make clothes, I make things for my home, and I make presents for other people. I teach my designs. I make and sell lots of my designs. I have three quilt tops sitting in a trunk waiting to be made up, two jackets cut out, one dress partially made, and several baby gifts that I must get done before this book goes to print. Not very much time passes between one person having a clear-out and giving me a bag of fabric or thread and me finding a bargain at a garage sale or charity shop.

In this book I want to pass on a few things I have come up with over my years of teaching quilting and craft making, although of course you don't need necessarily to make the exact same things as I show you here! Writing craft books isn't the way to get rich, so my reward will be seeing what you have made of my ideas. So send me pictures!

Your "fabric food chain"

In the classes I taught at Liberty's Sewing School I could always tell which of the wonderful ladies attending did not even have to think about money. They were the ones who, in my Scrap Craft classes, would cut the tiniest pattern piece right out of the centre of a large chunk of lovely Tana Lawn. I would catch the eye of other students, people like me who had spent time as a poor student (then more time married to a poor student) or been raised not to waste a thing, and we'd want to scream in despair. Setting aside the money-wasting, how about that fabric-wasting?!? It took me only a few classes to work out that giving my students the right-size piece of fabric for the project was what I would have to do to keep my blood pressure down. Some people like to save whales, I like to save fabric.

So what do I mean by "fabric food chain"? Well, I certainly don't mean that you have to use a particular scrap for a specific-size project only, but I would like you to consider the following: you have a square of fabric about 35cm (14in) square. Do you tear ALL of it up for use in a Rug canvas fabric project, or do you slice a 5cm (2in) strip off one side for four Sweet beads (page 30), use most of the rest for a Fabric Bowl (page 62), THEN use any left-over scraps for Rug canvas fabric (page 24) and Lazy crazy patchwork (page 22)? Nature has lined up all its creatures in an efficient manner, and I take the same approach to fabric. One of my fellow tutors at Liberty's used to say that "fabric starts to rot the minute it's put on the bolt after being woven", so you might as well put it to good use.

Sorting

If you make many different things, for example clothes and quilts and crafts and upholstery items, you tend to have a lot of different types of fabric. Some fabrics are suitable for lots of things, some for only a few, but you can help your fabric along a little by "evolving" it. I used to believe that the lightest fabric you could use for most crafts was cotton or cotton blends, but now I have seen the light and realize that far more lightweight fabrics can be used. Fusing two layers together, ironing on some interfacing, or backing an open-weave or lace piece, is all you need do to toughen up delicate fabrics and make them more suitable for some of the crafts in this book, such as the Fabric Bowls (page 62). Going the other way – making heavy fabric less thick and bulky – well, that's another matter, but there's no reason why you can't use some very thick bits of wool or velvet in a piece of Lazy crazy patchwork (LCP) (page 22) or some strips of it in Rug canvas fabric (RCF) (page 24). Also, a scrap of thick wool suiting worked perfectly for my Tassel project on page 88. You don't know until you try, and since it's only leftovers what have you got to lose?

There are three different methods of sorting. Usually I sort by weight and fabric content (see the pictures here and overleaf for ideas), but sorting by size or colour are also equally valid.

Weight and content

Thick wools and tartans, the somewhat less heavy velvets and velveteens, and glitzy fabrics such as sheers and lamés I group together as leftovers from dressmaking. Kept aside in a bag of their own are the many scraps of raw silk I've collected from the days of making bridesmaid dresses – I like to use those for machine-couching (page 34).

Thick wools and tartans

Velvets and velveteens

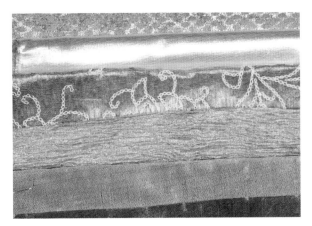
Sheers and lamés

Denim and bits of fabric left over from curtain- and cushion-making also get grouped together. As for cottons for quilting, I tend to divide them into prints and solids.

Size

I measure my biggest remnants, which I call "chunks", fold them neatly, and pin a piece of paper with the measurements written on it to a corner (like they do for remnant bins in stores). This way you'll know at a glance if a piece of fabric is going to be big enough for a certain project.

You can choose your own minimum measurement for this category or use mine: if it's bigger than 30cm (12in) it gets included in "chunks".

If it is an odd-shaped piece left over after I've cut out a dress, I trim off the weird little ends that you get when cutting clothes and put these pieces in with one of the smaller categories (see below).

Next, for me, come "nice pieces", and these would be between 10 and 30cm (4 and 12in) square. These are the pieces I'd use for fabric projects such as Fabric Bowls (page 62), Fabric Flowers (page 78), or perhaps part of an LCP Journal Cover (page 44). Of course "square" in my book doesn't really mean a four-sided shape with equal lengths – it is more of a guestimate of what that piece would be if it were square. Don't dwell too much on this, just make some size decisions that work for you.

All the small bits left over at the end I separate into three categories and store appropriately:
• Narrow strips of fabric: these would be 15cm (6in) long or more, yet less than 2.5cm (1in) wide, and I'd probably use them for RCF projects (see page 24 for the technique and start at page 46 for the projects themselves).
• Small squares: pieces roughly 5–7.5cm (2–3in) square, useful for Sweet beads (page 30), which go into their own tub.
• Everything else: pieces too small for Sweet beads or not long enough for RCF, the sort I'd use for LCP or a patchwork "Coffee Cuff" (page 50).

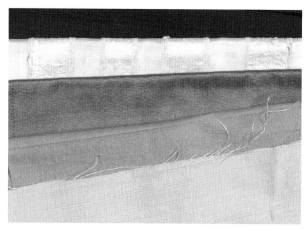

Silks

Denim and upholstery fabric

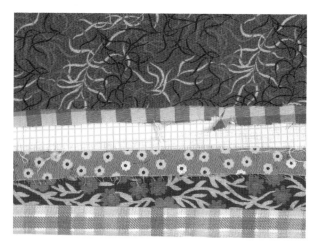

Cotton prints

Colour

If sorting by colour, I make a basic division of warm (reds, yellows, and oranges) and cool (blues, greens, and purples) colours. You could create quite specific groupings, such as "Christmas" (reds, greens, and golds) or pastels. Keeping some of my black and white (and all the tones inbetween) scraps together is a habit of mine, since I find that's a good colour combo for making crafts for guys (see page 56 for a Pencil Box I made for my better half).

Top tips

Don't throw out a piece of fabric faded by light – simply use it for the back of some LCP, or paint it with the method I talk about on page 19.

Thread

I buy just about any thread in any colour or make. For making large batches of rug canvas fabric I happily use overlock thread, and I am always on the hunt for bargain bags of threads in sale bins.

Since I also design needlepoint I'm not beyond incorporating some of my heavier wools and metallic threads into my crafts. I keep needlework threads that could also be used in crafts grouped together, yet still within my needlework store.

My new machine uses different bobbins from those for my poor, worn-out model, which seriously needed retiring. Instead of chucking out perfectly fine bobbins (keeping in mind that the

model that may one day replace my currently over-worked machine might be able to use those bobbins), I use them for storing ends of spools of thread. This way I can see just how much I have left of a colour, which isn't always easy to work out simply by looking at a spool.

I am NOT a pack-rat, nor do I have a compulsion to keep every last little bit of everything – but the very ends of spools or bobbins really CAN be useful, so in they go to a little ziplock bag and out they come at some time in the future to be used as flower stamens (which could be added to some Fabric Flowers, page 78), or as hair for a Juju (page 84 and see box, right).

Heavier wools and metallics can also be useful.

Collect a variety of coloured threads – you can never have too many.

A bobbin reveals how much thread you have left more easily than a spool, because you can't always tell the thread thickness (and therefore the amount there is left) from looking at a spool.

Top tip

If you come across a bag of thread at a car boot sale/garage sale/church jumble sale, ask politely if you can test it first before you buy it. Unwind a little piece, grasp it firmly and tug. If it breaks right away it isn't going to do you or your machine any good. As long as it works in my machine I will use older thread for decorative stitching, but I test it this way first to make sure.

Thread odds and ends

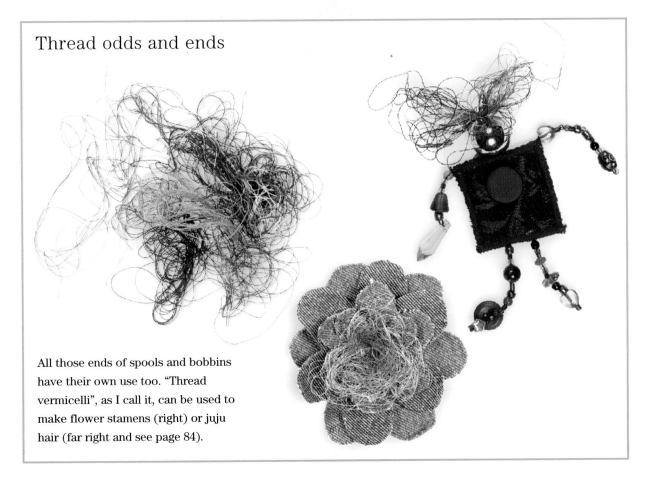

All those ends of spools and bobbins have their own use too. "Thread vermicelli", as I call it, can be used to make flower stamens (right) or juju hair (far right and see page 84).

Processing

There's sorting your fabric, then there's *processing* your fabric, which I think might be even more important for getting a grip on what you have and what you can use it on. We've all thrown a bit of clothing in the scrap bag with the thought that the colour or the fabric was quite nice and there might be something that you could do with it later, but often it sits and languishes when it really is an ugly duckling just waiting to be turned into a swan.

Dissecting a tie

1 Until you take a tie apart, you can't really get a sense of quite how much fabric goes into one. A quality tie will be held together at the back with one long thread, which is easily removed. You then have the whole length of fabric to play with.

2 The interfacing can go toward strengthening something like handles for the Leftover Fabric Bag (page 68), or if it is still on the "fluffy" side, shred it up for stuffing Sweet beads (page 30). The bits of lining can be used for rug canvas fabric scrap bags, which just leaves the label – for which I have yet to find a use!

Taking a sleeve apart

1 These heavy silk cap-style sleeves were removed from an antiques store find and relegated to the scrap bag.

2 Once taken apart they revealed a surprising amount of useable fabric, including an attractive reverse side.

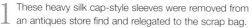

Recycling jeans

Denim crafts have been popular for a while, but I have to say that the items made with pristine denim off a roll from the fabric store rather miss the point. To my mind, if you want something to look like recycled jeans, there's nothing better than using the real thing. To get the most amount of usable fabric from a pair of clean old jeans, follow this formula.

1 Lay the jeans out flat and make the first cut up the inside of one leg, through the crotch and down the other leg.

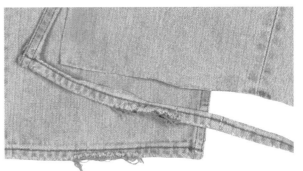

2 Trim off the thick folded seam from the inner legs and hems in one long piece.

3 From the bottom of the front zipper, make another cut along the edge all the way up to the waistline and right through.

4 Cut off the waistband and belt loops.

5 Cut out and discard the inner white pockets.

6 Now, either leave the jeans like this until you know what you want to do with them, or take out the front pockets and cut out the back pockets at this stage, to be left with plain old denim to continue cutting up for your chosen project.

Storage

What you store your fabric in depends on how much you have, of course, so I like to put things in containers relevant to their size. The bag the fabric came in is an obvious choice for larger pieces. Snip off an odd-shaped bit and fix it to the bag with a rough accounting of the quantity.

Film canisters

I don't think I will ever get a digital camera: film canisters are just too useful not to collect. These are ideal for sewing notions, a few beads left over from a jewellery project, buttons, or whatever fits. Tape a sample of the contents on the side or lid to indicate what's inside and to make sure you'll always have at least one to use.

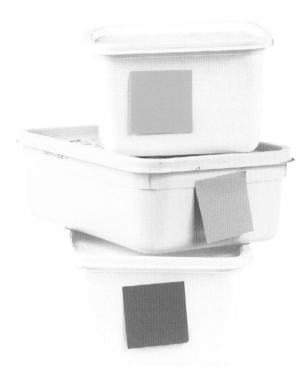

Colour-coded tubs

Medium and large ice-cream tubs are great for larger scraps: I use colour-coded sticky notes on the ends to label what I have in there. I note the date on which I made up the current contents (but only in pencil, since these tubs are merely a stop-over point on each piece of fabric's way to becoming something useful or beautiful).

Fabric rolls

Long strips of fabric, either precisely cut like these 5cm (2in) cotton strips, or long thin bits left over from cutting a pattern piece, stay relatively unwrinkled when wrapped around a cardboard tube. I cut up spent wrapping-paper tubes to just the size I need, or an empty toilet-paper roll holds two 5cm (2in) leftover quilt border pieces exactly.

Working storage

When you are selling your house you learn all about the concept of temporary storage when artfully arranging everything to make it look more attractive to buyers. The same applies to your fabric and craft supplies – you don't need everything all the time, but when you do you want to know where it all is. I call this "working storage".

Egg cartons neatly hold a selection of bits and pieces for the *projet du jour*. At the end of the day, close it up and everything is ready for the next session. Clear plastic tubs that can be stacked on top of each other are great for small fabric projects such as Sweet beads (page 30) or Fabric Flowers (page 78).

Checking your goodies

Shaking out the larger pieces to air them and rearranging your stock is a good way to get inspiration for projects, remind yourself that you really don't need the next scrap of black velvet you find in the remnant bin because you have enough already, and spark ideas about new colour combinations. Even if you don't have the time for crafting, still visit your fabric store occasionally.

Portable project kit

Don't you just hate it when life gets in the way of your stitching? Until there is a way to get things such as dentist appointments, while-you-wait car servicing, or travelling somewhere accomplished online, you are going to find yourself sitting around for a good portion of your life. Don't let it get to you, just use it as more time to stitch. If the situation requires it, replace your small scissors with one of the many little gadgets available for cutting threads (I found a great little ring a few years back and I've seen a couple of pendant types that also do the job), or bring along a dental floss box to save wear and tear on your teeth. The portable kit shown here was devised specifically for making Sweet beads (page 30).

Using your machine's stitches

To help me with designing, I have made up some little reference samples for the stitches on my current sewing machine (a Janome 3500 by the way). There's one for all the decorative stitches, one for zig-zag widths, and one for zig-zag lengths (see below). These really do come in handy, especially the zig-zag pair, when planning what you want to use for a project. You could write on the fabric which setting is which, but since I stitched one line for every width and length setting, all I do is count from one edge to know which one I need.

Reference stitch samples

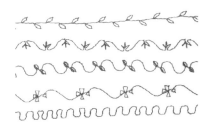

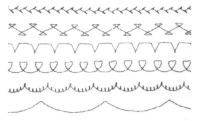

Decorative stiches

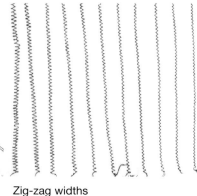

Zig-zag widths

Zig-zag lengths

Sewing machine advice

Here are my top five tips for taking care of your sewing machine, and not one involves having to take it to a shop and pay for the service.

1. Four out of five times a minor tension problem can be solved by re-threading the machine. I'm not kidding. Try it.

2. Snip the top thread and pull it through the machine works, which is how you should take out the thread all the time. It is worth losing 20cm (8in) of thread to pull it out *through* the machine rather than backward against all those little parts inside that you'll never see.

3. Remove the bobbin (and casing if that comes out) and blow on/into it every time you sew to get rid of little bits of fluff created by the thread rubbing against metal.

4. If you haven't used your machine in a while, start by running through a variety of stitches on a scrap of fabric to clear out any bits of dust or dirt.

5. Sharp needles are vital. I keep a sticker on the side of my machine where I write down when I put in a new needle. If I'm going to stitch a lot of rug canvas one week, I'll use a fresh needle after 30 hours or so of sewing, otherwise changing the needle once a month is sufficient.

Decorative stitching ideas

Lines of machine stitching are a great aid to blending together bits of fabric in the methods I'm going to show you on the following pages. (See LCP on page 22 and RCF on page 24.)

Top tips

Your machine's pre-set embroidery-style stitches can be used to liven up plain fabric, such as these pink stitches on some old pink crepe-back satin (A). A sheet of plastic covered in an assortment of stitches can be used on its own or layered over another piece of fabric (B).

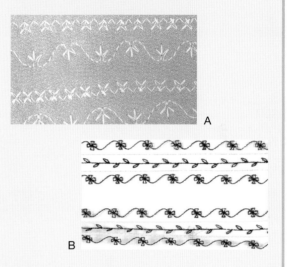

Do you have a little bit of fabric paint left over? Water it down a little and brush it onto plain calico (muslin). Leave it to dry, fix it according to the directions on the paint bottle, then run stitches over it (C and D). You can also use ordinary watercolour paint, which will need to be ironed on the reverse once dry to help fix it.

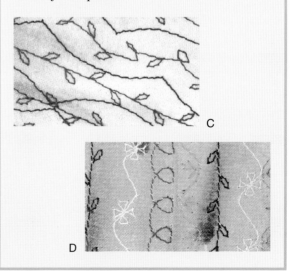

start
with what
you've got

Lazy Crazy Patchwork (LCP)

I was surprised to find out, back when I was learning to quilt, that the "crazy" of Victorian crazy patchwork was coined not due to the jumbled-up nature of the bits of fabric used but due to the fact that the end result resembled crazed porcelain (think of the crackled-looking background on an Oriental vase). When you consider the growing interest in textiles of the East (in both the USA and the UK) around the time this style of quilting was popular, and the industrial means of textile production, which meant that women could concentrate their needlework on the frivolous rather than the purely functional, you've got the grounds for a style of work that also took some advantage of the rapidly improving sewing machine. Surviving pieces from this era (a brief span of time during the late nineteenth century) tend to be items such as a throw or bedcover that covered only the top of a mattress.

You can use my fast method (hence the "lazy") to make pieces of patchwork for the projects that follow, which are quite small, but if you want to go for bigger projects might I suggest making 30–35cm (12–14in) squares from the following method. You can then make those into whatever size you want.

I use a machine for assembling the bits and pieces of fabric and at the same time add the decorative topstitching that is so characteristic of crazy patchwork. No handstitching is involved here, unless I want to add a few beads or buttons at the end.

It isn't strictly necessary to know what you are going to make out of a piece of LCP when you form it. In fact, you might get inspiration only after you make a few samples.

Fast-method patchwork

1 I've used a strip of 5cm (2in) white cotton fabric for a base, on to which I've pinned assorted scraps of fancy fabrics. Since you cover the whole of the backing material, you can use whatever you like for it – perhaps some really weird print you don't like and know you'd never use, or a bit of fabric with a stain on it that will not come out. For the top layer, sheer fabric scraps look great straddled over two or more solid fabrics.

Top tips

If you do know what you are going to make, I'd advise making the pieces slightly bigger by about 20 per cent, since all the topstitching can have a shrinking effect on the base fabric. It isn't anything to worry about, but you should keep it in mind as you plan out what you need.

Any scraps that get cut off can be made into Sweet beads (page 30) or incorporated into yet another piece of Lazy crazy patchwork.

2 Sew three to four lines of stitching to fasten the little scraps securely to the base, then remove the pins.

3 Now you can machine-couch cord or ribbon to it (page 34) until you are satisfied with the result.

4 If you want to neaten up the edges, sew strips of coordinating fabric along each edge. This isn't necessary if you are just playing around and don't have a project in mind.

Rug Canvas Fabric (RCF)

If you think that your scraps are too long and thin and even raggedy to seem useful, think again my friend. Using sturdy rug canvas (which is often less than half the price of needlepoint canvas) as a base, you can weave those raggedy scraps in and out then machine stitch over them until you have an all-new piece of funky "patchwork", which I call Rug canvas fabric, or RCF for short. You can then make this into all sorts of accessories, gifts, and jewellery. Full instructions for making RCF are on page 26.

The canvas

The type of canvas used for this technique is three and a half holes per inch. It is commonly called rug canvas since this size is also used for some rug-hooking projects. If you don't have a local shop that carries it, plenty of online stores do. Sometimes blue lines run through the canvas, which can affect your fabric colour choice. I get around this by using a blue or cool colour scheme.

Fabrics to use

I have used both the lightest chiffon and the heaviest wool in the samples you see here; all you need to keep in mind is the width of the strips. A very fine light fabric can be up to 2.5cm (1in) wide, while a thick chunky suiting needs to be just about the width of the holes of the canvas. You can also stitch two short scrap pieces together to get one long enough to weave through the canvas size you've chosen.

I have stretched my definition of "fabric" when it comes to this particular technique. Binding left over from quilt projects is made of fabric, so I cut scraps of that lengthwise as needed. Thicker cords from needlecraft projects can be quite wide, but as long as they will pass under the foot of my sewing machine, I use them. Offcuts of ribbon can also be used, again cut to the desired thickness.

Colour choices

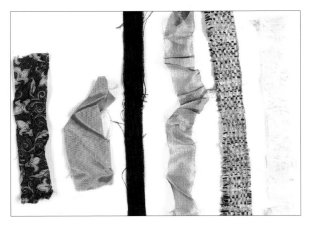

The strip second from the right inspired the colour choices of the rest of my selection.

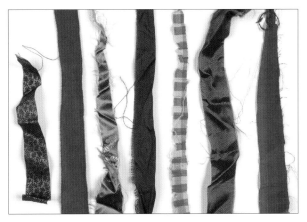

If you use a lot of one colour in your own crafts or clothes, try putting all of those together.

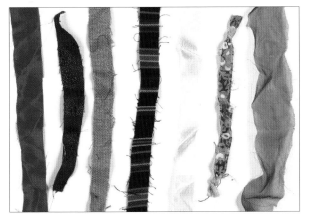

All warms or cools is another option.

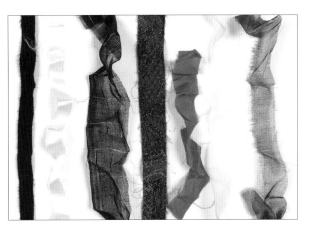

Even black and white needn't be too "black and white" if you sneak in some fabrics with metallic threads.

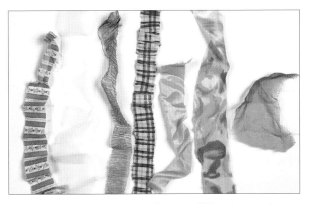

Sometimes the project you choose will inspire a colour theme: these bright and subtle pastels became an RCF picture frame (page 72) for a baby whose gender was kept under wraps.

Weaving and stitching RCF

The sturdy yet flexible nature of Rug canvas fabric becomes apparent only once you've made a piece of it yourself. What I'll show you on these two pages is the basic technique, but feel free to add in bits of lace or cord or other trims in place of (or along with) your fabric strips. Once you've mastered the technique you will need to turn to the project section, which starts on page 42, for a wide selection of ideas on what you can make.

While I am happy for you to plunge right into one of the many projects that use this technique, I'll tell you now that a few samples first to get the hang of it are really worth your time. They give

you the perfect opportunity to play with colour combinations or add thread, cord, or ribbon. The pieces won't be wasted – you can use them later on for jewellery or as trim for larger projects. Experiment, too, with the best needle for the stitching: you will need at least a 14, if not a 16.

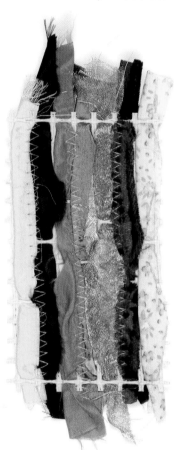

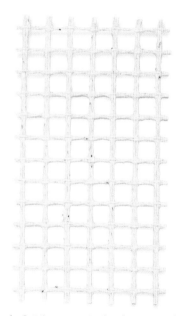

1 Cut the canvas to the size you need plus an extra hole or two all around.

2 Weave the fabric through the holes as shown (no need to go through every hole). Always leave a little extra at either end because as you machine stitch over the canvas the fabric can pucker slightly, and you do not want the ends to come loose.

3 Once you have woven the whole piece, choose a thread that will blend with the fabric and set your machine to a very wide and very long zig-zag stitch. All you are doing at this stage is holding down the fabric, so stitch between pairs of fabric-strip rows on the first pass, always trying to straddle the canvas.

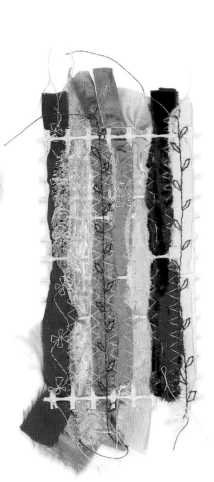

4 With another colour thread, continue to stitch down the fabric where it was not touched the first time. Resist using fancy stitches until you have a base of flattened fabric strips.

5 Now feel free to go crazy. I like to mix up geometric and flower stitches, but you can keep to just one or the other.

6 Somehow I just know when I have put enough stitches in. You don't want it to look too crowded or cluttered, so that's why I suggest you make up a few sample bits like this first to get the hang of it – there are lots of things you'll be able to make with them so they won't be wasted.

From your very first test piece you can make your very first project. See page 76 for a little fold-over case or page 91 for some jewellery ideas.

Backing RCF

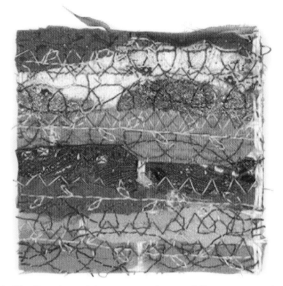

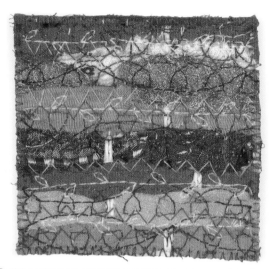

1 Trim the edges of the canvas so that a solid line runs around the fabric shape, as shown. If the canvas has a curvy shape just trim as neatly as you can.

2 If the edges are especially scraggly you can run a line of zig-zag stitching around the edge before the next step.

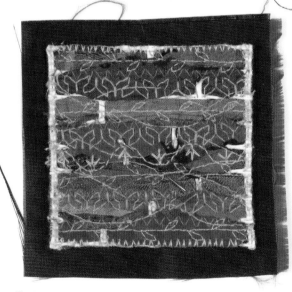

3 Cut a piece of your chosen lining a little bit bigger than your shape, then pin them together, wrong sides facing.

4 Using a zig-zag stitch of a medium length and width, sew all around the edge of the piece. You might find that the lining rolls itself along the edge a bit as you stitch it on, but that's perfectly fine.

5 After sewing once all the way around, trim the lining close and add additional layers of zig-zag stitch (vary the length if you like) until the edge is nice and clean. Try not to start each row of zig-zag at the same corner.

6 I find that four passes generally does the trick, but it will depend on the length of the stitches. For some projects you will be sewing finished pieces together (see Boxes, page 52), so keep that in mind when making your thread colour choices.

Top tip

Once you've made six squares you can make a lidded box (page 52). Add one more and the lid can be pagoda-style.

Fabric for backing

My first quilting teacher told us always to use the best quality fabric for the back of your work. It shouldn't matter that "nobody is going to see it": YOU know it's there. As for plain or patterned, matching or contrasting, use whatever you fancy.

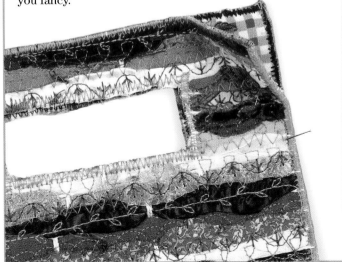

Sweet beads

Sweet beads were the development of "No-cal Candy" (page 82), and both were inspired by a silk sample book. Both projects start in the same way, but the highly versatile beads are a sort of tucked-in version of the candy.

This slightly more useful version of the two techniques can best be described as a mouse-sized bolster cushion, to which you can add all sorts of decoration and turn it into a little work of art. Jewellery (page 90) and Tassels (page 88) that use the beads follow, along with suggestions on how to use beads to decorate other projects in the book, but why not make up a bowl of these basic forms first so you have plenty to choose from? I keep a little box of sewn tubes at hand and work on them while watching TV.

This is also a great travel project: make up lots of tubes, cut them to size, and stuff a big handful of wadding (batting) into a ziplock bag or small plastic tub. You can keep yourself occupied for hours at 10,000m (35,000ft) making the beads. The travel kit on page 17 is the first thing I pack!

Making the beads

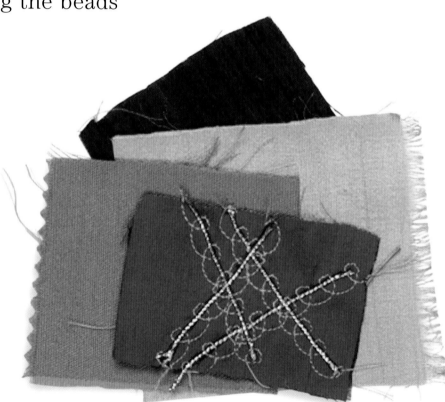

1 This is the time to get out that little bag of nice tiny scraps that you have stashed away. All you need is a minimum size of around 5cm (2in) square (at any rate, try this size for your first couple while you get the hang of it). I sometimes do a little machine stitching on my bits first, either some plain decorative topstitching or maybe a little machine-couching (page 34).

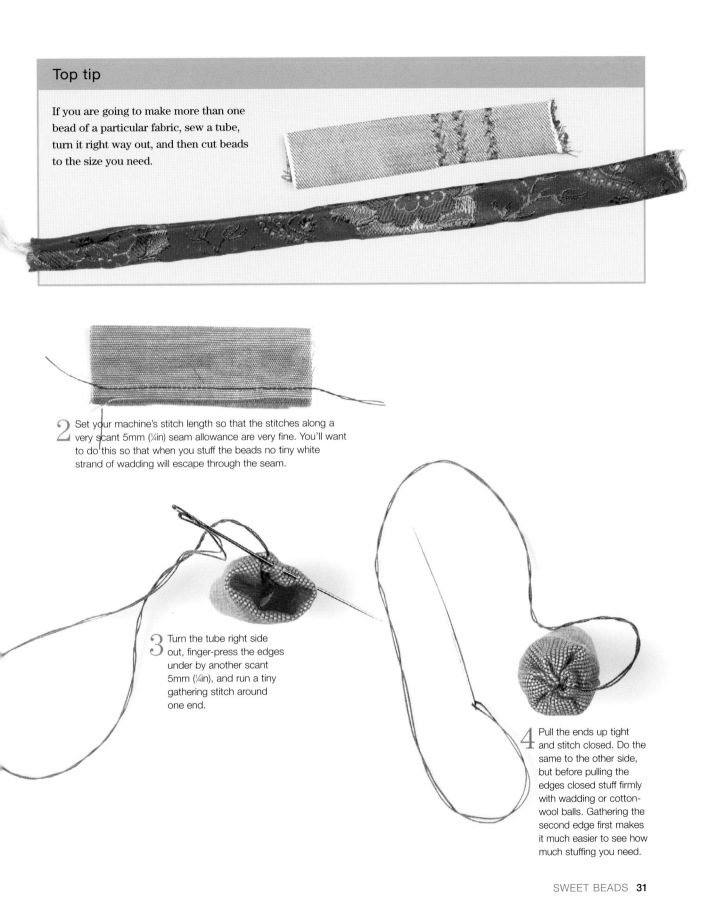

Top tip

If you are going to make more than one bead of a particular fabric, sew a tube, turn it right way out, and then cut beads to the size you need.

2 Set your machine's stitch length so that the stitches along a very scant 5mm (¼in) seam allowance are very fine. You'll want to do this so that when you stuff the beads no tiny white strand of wadding will escape through the seam.

3 Turn the tube right side out, finger-press the edges under by another scant 5mm (¼in), and run a tiny gathering stitch around one end.

4 Pull the ends up tight and stitch closed. Do the same to the other side, but before pulling the edges closed stuff firmly with wadding or cotton-wool balls. Gathering the second edge first makes it much easier to see how much stuffing you need.

Decorating the beads

You can leave your beads plain until you decide what to do with them, or start decorating and figure their use out later.

A clean plastic fruit-salad tub is a great place to store beads awaiting decoration.

A few seed beads left over from some other craft project might have stumped you as to what to use them for, but just a few are needed to decorate these tiny stuffed forms.

Sometimes I have just the right bead or beads to decorate only one end. But that's okay: something will suggest itself for the other end soon enough.

Little pieces of coloured wire, with or without seed beads, add interest and texture.

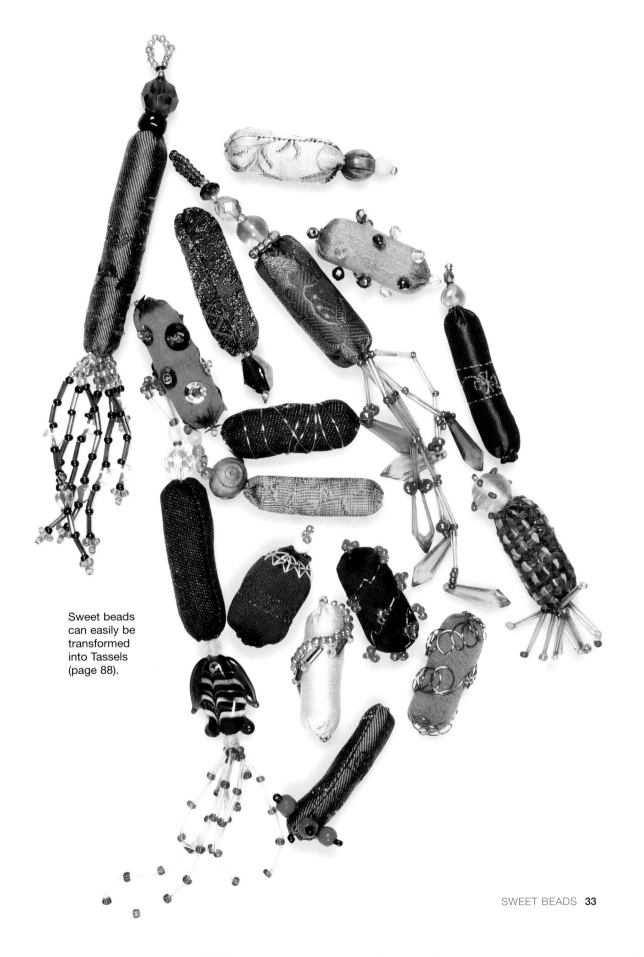

Sweet beads
can easily be
transformed
into Tassels
(page 88).

Machine-couching

So many machines have a slew of fancy stitches that never get used, but now is your chance for some experimentation. A scrap bit of fabric is the perfect ground for this straightforward method for attaching cord and ribbon.

"Couching" merely means using thread to attach a thicker thread or cord to a piece of fabric. I used the technique all the time while stitching my goldwork projects when I spent a year studying at the Royal School of Needlework . Thankfully for you, this machine version is a heck of a lot faster.

If you have a specific project in mind, say the bag on page 70, make sure to cut the fabric a little bigger than you actually need. The more lines of couching you stitch, the more the fabric will "shrink" from having rows of thread put through it. Leaving about 2.5cm (1in) on all sides should be enough, but if you aren't sure leave more space. (If it's too big you can always cut it smaller, but if you left too little space to begin with, you can't cut it bigger!)

I like to lay the cord I am couching a little farther than the edge of the fabric so I can just get hold of it when putting the fabric under the foot of the machine. The same is true for the other end – in fact, I leave the cord or ribbon uncut until I get about two-thirds of the way down whatever is being couched. If you do this you have less chance of coming up a little short on the end. You can neaten everything up afterwards, so don't worry about the ends.

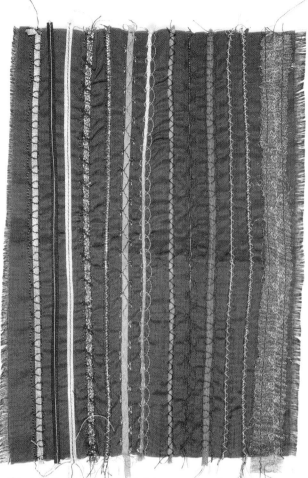

Straight lines of couched ribbon and cord

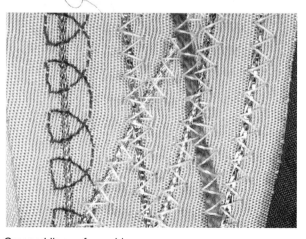

Crossed lines of couching

Using machine-couching

Why not combine machine-couching with your machine's decorative stitches (page 18). You'll be amazed at the variety of effects you can achieve.

On Lazy crazy patchwork (page 22) or…

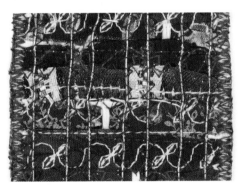

Rug canvas fabric (page 24), or try…

on clear plastic…

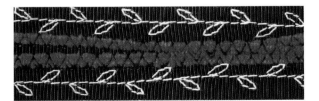

or on grosgrain ribbon.

Top tip

The way I achieved this sunken-in look was by taking an old bit of light-faded fabric, laying a scrap of wadding (batting) on top and placing the fabric I wanted to machine-couch on top of that. (This is more or less how you machine-quilt.)

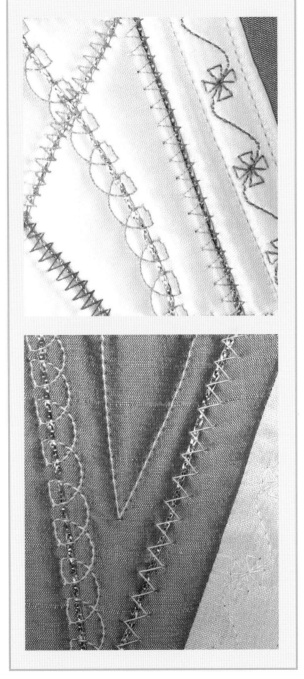

Machine-wrap Cord

If your machine can do a zig-zag stitch, you can whip up a batch of this cord in no time at all. Depending on the width of the cord (shown here is size two/size 50, which I like best), set your machine's width for a zig-zag stitch just a little wider than the cord itself. If you have the ability to lower the feed dogs on the machine do so, as this allows you to control the speed at which the cord passes through the running machine. If not don't worry, you can adjust the stitch length and that works just as well.

Have a look at the stitch samplers I made from my current machine's selection of widths and lengths on page 18. For me, the 4.5 size works best. If you aren't sure which width to use on

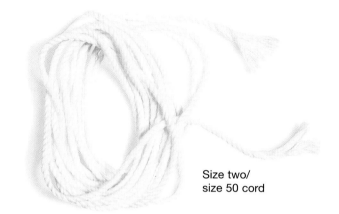

Size two/
size 50 cord

your machine, stitch a few centimetres (inches) on a scrap of fabric and lay your cord on top to judge. You don't want the needle to pierce the cord, only go from side to side of it.

Making the cord

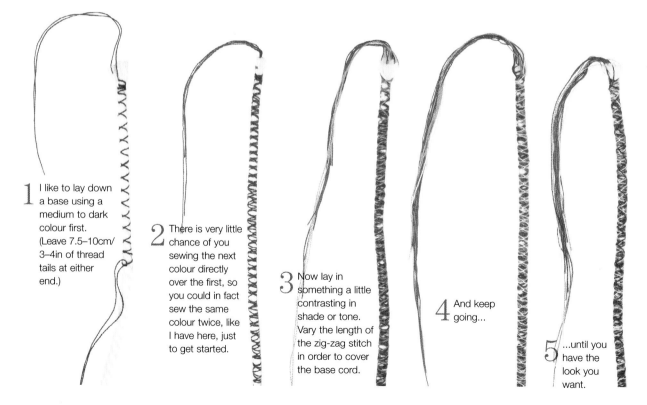

1 I like to lay down a base using a medium to dark colour first. (Leave 7.5–10cm/ 3–4in of thread tails at either end.)

2 There is very little chance of you sewing the next colour directly over the first, so you could in fact sew the same colour twice, like I have here, just to get started.

3 Now lay in something a little contrasting in shade or tone. Vary the length of the zig-zag stitch in order to cover the base cord.

4 And keep going...

5 ...until you have the look you want.

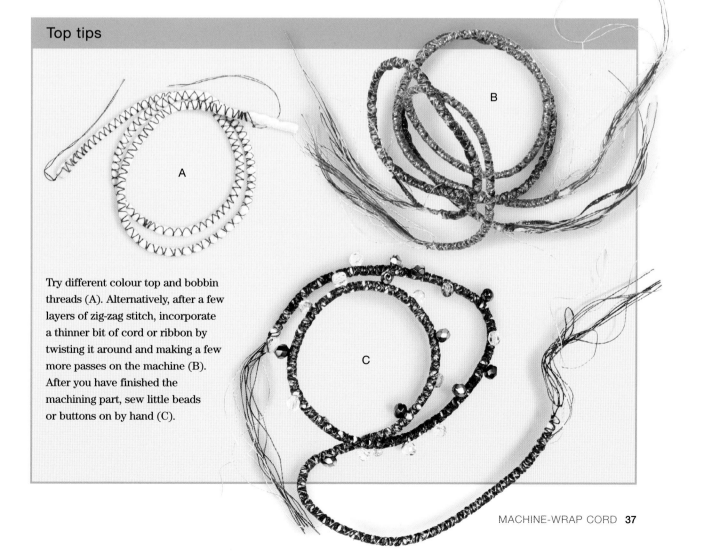

What's rather cool is that the more layers of thread you sew on the cord, the better it will hold its shape when you bend it.

Top tips

Try different colour top and bobbin threads (A). Alternatively, after a few layers of zig-zag stitch, incorporate a thinner bit of cord or ribbon by twisting it around and making a few more passes on the machine (B). After you have finished the machining part, sew little beads or buttons on by hand (C).

I like to keep a few metre (yard) lengths of cord by my machine when I am dressmaking. If I like the colour I am using, or there's only a bit left on the top thread and/or bobbin, I pass a length of cord through a few times. I don't always finish it off completely but save it for later and add other colours once I know what I am going to use it for.

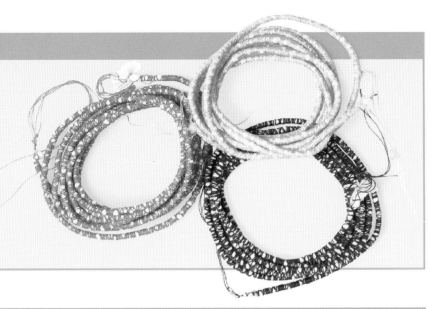

Another use for beads

Make your machine-wrap cord a little more interesting by taking advantage of its lovely "curvability". Of course, you can just make up lots of lengths of combinations and think about what to do with them later! See pages 81 and 92 for some specific projects using machine-wrap cord.

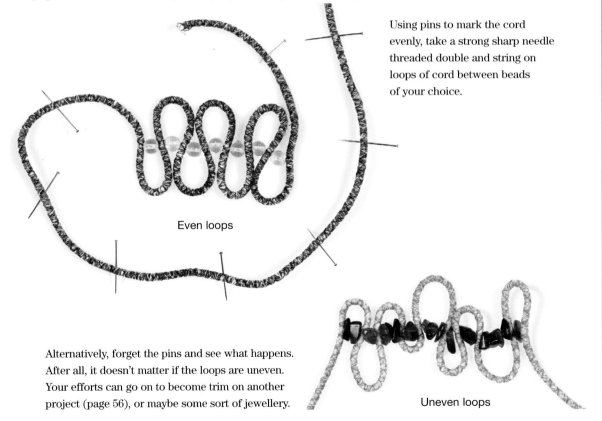

Using pins to mark the cord evenly, take a strong sharp needle threaded double and string on loops of cord between beads of your choice.

Even loops

Alternatively, forget the pins and see what happens. After all, it doesn't matter if the loops are uneven. Your efforts can go on to become trim on another project (page 56), or maybe some sort of jewellery.

Uneven loops

Ruched Fabric

Quite often you have nice long strips left over either from quilting or dressmaking where you had to cut out some long pattern pieces. This is a part-hand, part-machine method.

Ruching the strips

1 Start with a long scrap of fabric at least 5cm (2in) wide. With the right sides together, stitch along the longest edge then turn right side out. If you want sharper edges, you need a light touch of the iron; finger pressing gives you a softer edge.

2 Stitch a series of triangles, as shown, across the fabric strip with doubled thread.

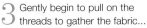

3 Gently begin to pull on the threads to gather the fabric...

4 ...until you have this! These make great handles for the Leftover Fabric Bag (page 68), or see page 81 for how to turn them into one of my three styles of Fabric Flowers.

Quilter's scrunchies

Since we're working with long thin scraps, I'll give you my two-colour scrunchie recipe. The minimum fabric length you'll need is 90cm (35in).

1 I've found that the optimum scrunchie starting width is 9cm (3½in), so two 5cm (2in) contrasting strips meet that requirement when you sew them right sides together along one long edge. Then sew along the other long edge, but start and finish stitching about 5cm (2in) in from the ends.

2 Turn the tube right-side out, using either one of those long thin turning tools or a safety pin pinned to one end so you can work the tube through itself.

3 Pin, then sew the short ends right sides together. Insert a 20cm (8in) piece of elastic through the gap, stitch the elastic ends together, then slipstitch the fabric to close.

Add some Fabric Flowers (page 78) for a finishing touch.

Button Blooms

These naïve Button blooms can be used in all sorts of ways: around the edge of an RCF frame, stuck in a green leafy plant lacking its own flowers, or stitched to a handmade paper card.

Yes, I know, it isn't exactly a fabric leftover project, but don't you tell me that you, as a fabric hoarder, do not have stray buttons lurking about that you'd like a use for.

Making the blooms

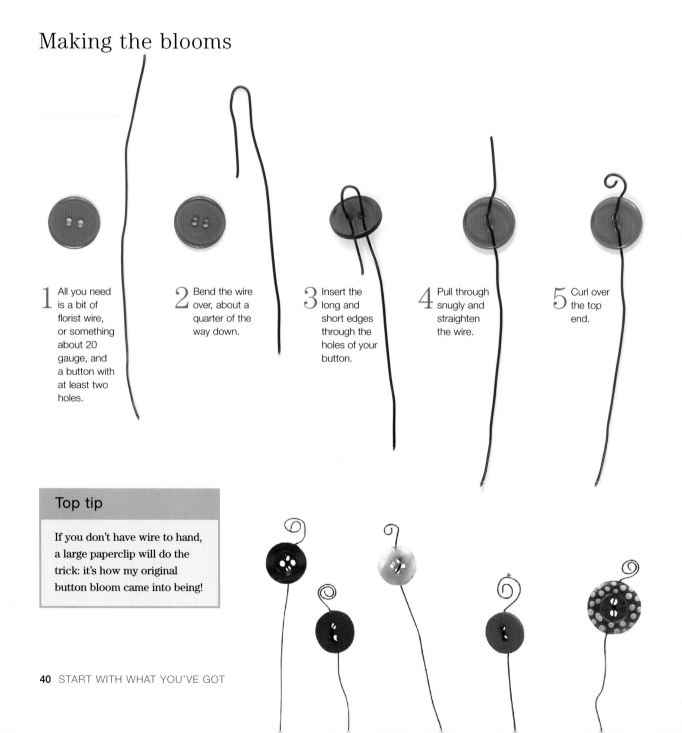

1 All you need is a bit of florist wire, or something about 20 gauge, and a button with at least two holes.

2 Bend the wire over, about a quarter of the way down.

3 Insert the long and short edges through the holes of your button.

4 Pull through snugly and straighten the wire.

5 Curl over the top end.

Top tip

If you don't have wire to hand, a large paperclip will do the trick: it's how my original button bloom came into being!

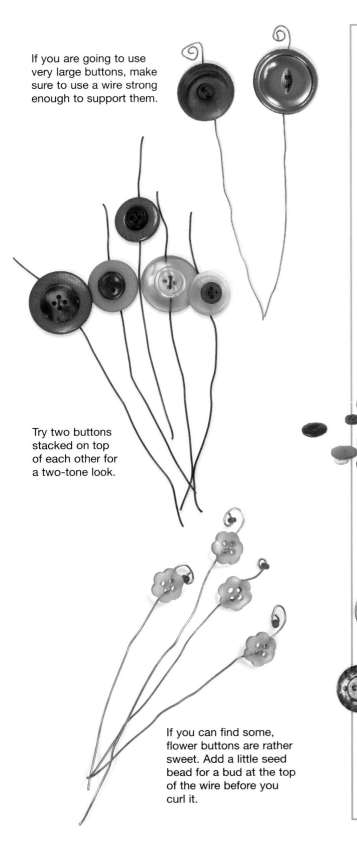

If you are going to use very large buttons, make sure to use a wire strong enough to support them.

Try two buttons stacked on top of each other for a two-tone look.

If you can find some, flower buttons are rather sweet. Add a little seed bead for a bud at the top of the wire before you curl it.

Nail-polish buttons

If you like the look of the painted buttons I have scattered throughout the book but don't want to invest in paint and brushes for a one-off project, why not go to your dressing table or bathroom and collect all your bottles of nail polish. You have a built-in brush with perfect consistency paint. Once your design is dry, seal it with clear polish. You might want to practise first on a bit of paper to get the drops of polish just right.

what
you can
make

Journal Cover

■ Techniques used: Lazy crazy patchwork (page 22)

If you like keeping a journal, turn an inexpensive blank book into a personalized place for recording your thoughts. Why not use scraps of fabric which hold special memories? You can also use this method to cover a small photo album. If you want to make a journal out of RCF, see page 48.

1 Measure the height of the book and add 2cm (¾in), then measure around the book and add 13cm (5in). These are your measurements for the book cover. I know it seems as though it will be too wide, but trust me: the short ends will be folded over to make the pockets. This project is a good way to highlight a bit of LCP you've made up. Here I have a strip inserted between light blue chambray left over from a skirt.

2 Once you've cut your fabric to size, cut an identical piece of lining fabric (which of course doesn't have to be lining fabric, if you know what I mean). Pin with right sides together and stitch right around the edges using a scant 5mm (¼in) seam allowance. Then make a vertical cut in the very centre of the lining fabric, just enough to turn the cover right side out.

3 Press the cover lightly around the edges. Place the binding of the journal over the centre of the cover and wrap the short ends around the front and back covers, checking that the fabric is loose enough to allow the book to close. Pin in place, then hand stitch these side pockets at top and bottom.

Top tips

You can either slipstitch the vertical cut closed or fuse a bit of fabric over the hole.

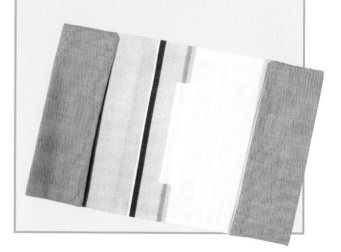

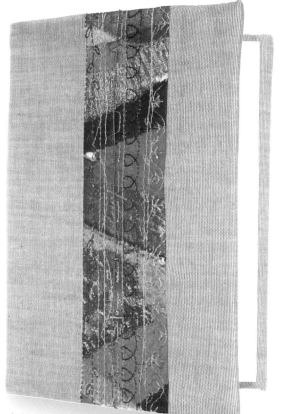

4 Slip the book into the finished cover.

A LCP journal cover

Instead of using just a strip of LCP, why not use LCP for the whole cover? A piece I had made up already wasn't quite the right size, so I added some satin to the ends and then ran a row of stitching down the edge to help blend the solid fabric with the stitched.

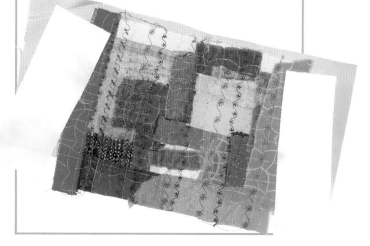

Decorating bought journals

■ Techniques used: Rug canvas fabric and Button blooms (pages 24 and 40)

If you want to make the fastest gift ever, just trim an attractive bought journal with some of the many bits and pieces I've shown you how to make. Simply attach some Button blooms or some of the scraps of Rug canvas fabric used in the Jewellery project (page 91) with craft glue. You could also stitch a Sweet bead (page 30) to a bit of ribbon and glue it into the spine for a "no-lose" bookmark (page 49).

Notecard Folio

■ Techniques used: Rug canvas fabric (page 24)

Even in this age of email there are some things that require writing by hand, and I have found these notecard folios are a great gift for the fair number of folk I know who have no use for computers. This is a very easy project for your first RCF project because it uses only one piece.

This was one of the first items I made after perfecting the technique of RCF. I knew that the sturdy nature of the new technique I'd devised would be good for boxes, and I'd had some ideas about jewellery, but I wanted to have a whole range of RCF items to sell at my assorted craft outlets. A friend's birthday was coming up and I'd got her some attractive cards at the British Museum that came in pretty packaging, and it was that packaging that inspired the folios.

I suggest you acquire your notecards first before undertaking this project. It would be rather annoying to put time and effort into a folio like this then not be able to find the right size and colour card. Let the colour of the cards you've found inspire your colour choice for the folio.

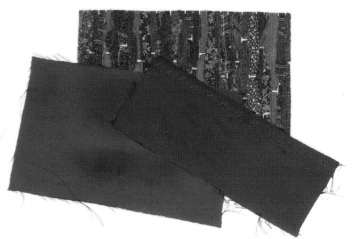

2 Weave and stitch the RCF, trim, then cut two pieces of fabric for the lining and the pocket. The lining should be the same size as the cover, and the pocket should be the same width but only about three-quarters of the height. Of course they don't need to be the same colour.

1 Lay out your cards and envelopes on a piece of RCF. Cut to size, leaving at least one hole of extra canvas space around the cards and envelopes.

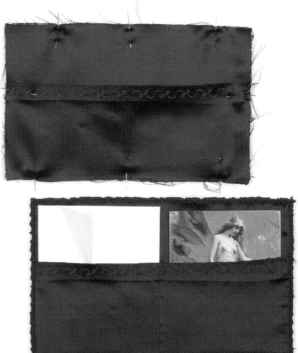

3 Fold the top of the pocket piece over twice and finish the edge with a plain or decorative stitch. Line up the centres of the fabric, the lining, and the pocket and pin them together. Then make one pass around the edge using zig-zag stitch. Create a dividing line in the pocket by stitching through all three layers. Continue zig-zagging the edge until it is finished.

Top tip

When making the initial
measurement, you could add
a little extra to the width to
create a thin pocket down
the middle for a pen.

4 By hand, stitch on
ribbon ties to keep
the folio closed.

Alternative journal cover method

Using the Notecard Folio method of separate
pockets enables you to make a journal cover
out of RCF, which is too bulky to turn over for
pockets. This picture shows the inner workings
of a RCF journal – with two side pockets to slip
the journal into rather than the single pocket
across the bottom as for the Folios. The pockets,
made out of the lining fabric, should be the same
height as the journal and each 5cm (2in) wide
once it is finished neatly. Layer the pieces and
stitch the edges as in step 3 on page 44.

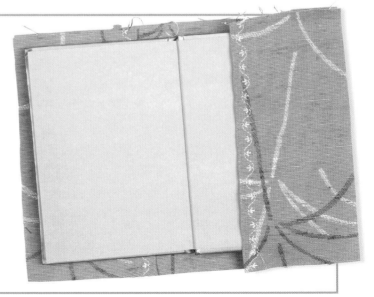

Bookmarks

■ Techniques used: Rug canvas fabric and Sweet beads (pages 24 and 30)

Grosgrain, silk, or sheer ribbon (with the ends folded over to keep them from fraying) are all a suitable choice for these bookmarks, which are an excellent present to give to a book lover, perhaps along with a book voucher.

A strip of Rug canvas fabric would also make a bookmark that you could trim with any of the options shown here. If you use fancy fabric you might not feel the need to decorate, but if you use a fairly plain piece of RCF then some eye-catching decoration would provide the finishing touch.

Greetings cards

■ Techniques used: Rug canvas fabric and Button blooms (pages 24 and 40)

Handmade paper cards are a very nice background for some of the smaller techniques. Make sure they are sturdy enough to hold the weight of Button blooms or Jujus (page 84). Stitch the Button blooms to the card with clear thread, as I have, or use stranded cotton to make embroidered grass and leaves. The Juju on the cream card is actually a pin you can remove, so the card is a present as well!

"Coffee Cuffs"

While making up the first dozen or so test versions of these "cuffs", I discovered there is a fine line between form and function. You want them to be interesting, but not difficult or uncomfortable to hold. Of course, you also need to keep in mind their main job, which is to keep you safe from the burning hot java variations like the boring cardboard ones do!

You can either use the template provided on page 95 or draft your own from a cardboard cuff at your local coffee shop. I have tried my template on the major brands, though, and because of the sort of bias cut that results from the shape, there is a certain amount of give. It should fit fine regardless of brand or cup size.

The heaviest polyester wadding (batting) you can use for the inner layer is 50g (2oz). I've also made these with Warm and Natural cotton (one or two layers – your choice). A cotton or cotton blend seems to work best for the lining fabric.

2 The lining and wadding should be a little bigger, too. Lay the lining right side down, add the wadding, and then the cuff itself, right side up.

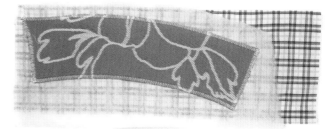

3 Pin them together at a few points and then zig-zag all the way around once.

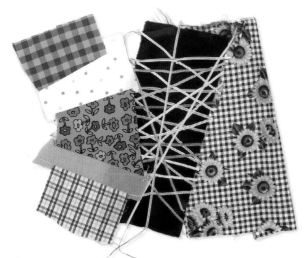

1 Whatever fabric you are going to use for your cuff, remember to cut it a bit larger if you are going to embellish it first with machine-couching (page 34) or decorative machine stitches (page 18). Using the template on page 95, cut out the outside of the cuff.

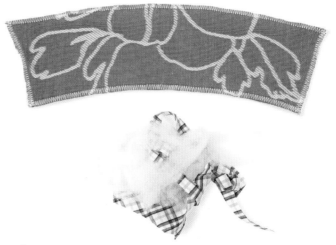

4 Trim the edges evenly and start the next row of zig-zag from a different corner – go all the way around again. (Of course, you'll save the bits you've trimmed: fabric for RCF and bits of wadding to stuff your Sweet beads.)

5 Add as many levels of stitches as you like, but when it comes to the last batch of zig-zag stitches, stitch only along the top and bottom edges.

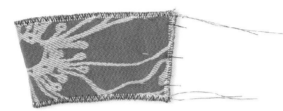

6 Pin the short ends together, shorten the zig-zag stitch a little, and topstitch the ends to close.

A variety of cuffs

You could make a whole range of cuffs to suit your mood and time of day, or the type of coffee/ hot beverage you're drinking. I'd have a caramel mocha in the blue version with couching, but some nice comforting hot chocolate with whipped cream in the patchwork one.

Boxes

■ Technique used: Rug canvas fabric (page 24)

Square box

This is the easiest of all the boxes in the book, and to some extent all the variations that follow use similar methods. Once you've made some square boxes (and the boxes on the pages to come), you might find it easier to weave and stitch a large piece of RCF and then cut it into the smaller size pieces that you require.

Decorative boxes are unusual items in that they are both a great gift and great packaging; in fact, if you make them pretty enough, the boxes might be more appreciated than any shop-bought gifts inside. With fitted or pagoda-style lids, and Sweet bead handles, who could resist them?

2 Pin two sections, wrong sides together, along one side and use a medium-length zig-zag stitch to sew them together. Note that one side of the zig-zag needs to go through the two pieces and the other should land outside the edges.

3 Following the same method, sew four sections together to form a cube.

1 To make a basic box you'll need six backed squares of Rug canvas fabric. I have found that a square box that measures more than about 18cm (7in) along the edge starts to get a little floppy, so for your first box might I suggest one that is at least half that size.

4 While you can use the machine to add the bottom and lid, I find that hand sewing is a little less fiddly and really doesn't take that much longer. The bottom needs to be sewn all the way around but the lid needs sewing on one side only.

Square boxes are just perfect for storing Sweet beads (page 30) and Tassels (page 88).

Nested set

If you are feeling quite adventurous, you could make a set of three or five (or more) boxes that nest inside each other, Russian doll-style. I'd make each box for this option at least three holes smaller than the next size, especially if you are going to use Sweet beads as lid handles.

Box uses

This set of small boxes was made to fit into a dresser drawer to hold cuff-links, bracelets, and rings. The labels on these lids are bits of handmade paper, which can be stitched on with leftover ends of embroidery cotton (floss). If you want to change the contents, just change the labels. There's not enough room here for me to list all the things I use my boxes for.

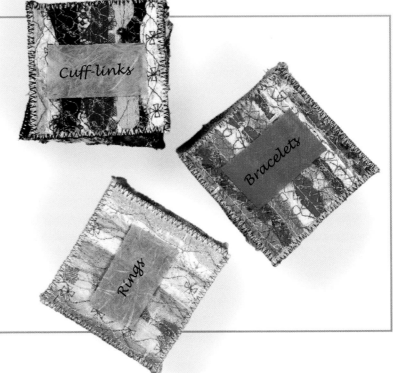

Fitted lid

Instead of attaching a hinged lid, as on page 53, you could make a separate fitted lid for a square box. This turns it into an especially good gift box, since all you need do is tie a bit of ribbon around it, add a gift tag, and hope that the present inside is as appreciated as your box!

3 Weave and stitch the lid piece in the colours and stitches of the box it is for (unless you fancy a contrast). Back the edges of the lid, stitching around all the indented corners.

1 For this type of lid, you'll need a piece of rug canvas that is four squares higher and four squares wider than the side and bottom pieces of the box it is for.

4 Draw the edges together at the corners and firmly stitch closed.

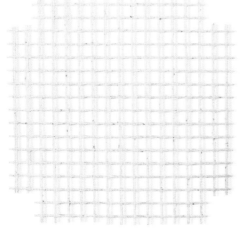

2 Cut out one complete square from each corner of the larger square of canvas as shown here.

5 Place the lid on the box, and admire. I don't think this style of box needs much in the way of extra adornment, but, as always, it's up to you.

One-piece box

You can adapt the fitted-lid method (page 55) to create a larger, one-piece, open-top box (or, by adding a handle, a basket). Once I have cut RCF into specific shapes for other projects, I often have good size square or rectangular pieces left that lend themselves to this project.

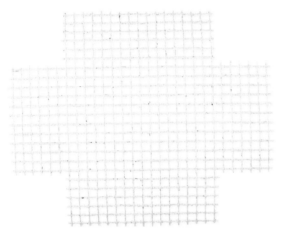

1 Follow the instructions on page 55, but at step 2 make the corner cuts larger than instructed to form higher sides. Make sure that all the squares you cut out are the same size. Once you have sewn it together as detailed in step 4, the lid can be reversed to become an open-top box.

2 Adding a strip of RCF as a handle like this, turns the box into a basket.

Decorative edging

■ Techniques used: Rug canvas fabric and Machine-wrap cord (pages 24 and 36)

Randomly stitch loops of machine-wrap cord along the edge of one of these one-piece boxes and you won't need any other trim. The black-and-white colour scheme makes it more "guy-friendly", don't you think? I like to make crafts for the men in my life, but it's no good if your husband/dad/brothers doesn't feel comfortable putting it on their desk at work.

Pagoda-style lid

This lid requires two squares of Rug canvas fabric. Weave, stitch, and back the squares to match the five you needed to make the box (see page 53). The oriental style of this lid gives a hint of Eastern promise to a standard square box.

1 Cut both squares in half on the diagonal.

3 With the lined sides facing, zig-zag stitch the two pairs of triangles together so that when you open them out each pair will look like this. Then sew those two pieces together along the long edge to form the box lid.

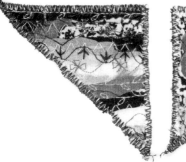

2 Finish the raw edges and turn each pair, like this.

Top tip

If you want an even more peaked roof, instead of cutting the two roof squares the same size as the box sides cut them three to four squares bigger. Then follow the directions above.

Triangle box

I started you off with a standard square box, to which you can now add one or two different lids, depending on your mood, but now we're moving on to different box shapes, here and overleaf. A triangle box requires five squares of the same size. Once you have decided on the size, weave and stitch the Rug canvas fabric.

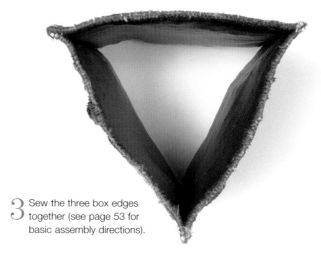

1 Back three of the squares (see page 28), but for the remaining two squares finish only one of the edges, since these will be cut into the triangle base and lid (see Top tip page 59). Use a pin to mark the centre of the opposite unfinished side.

3 Sew the three box edges together (see page 53 for basic assembly directions).

2 Carefully cut from one finished corner to the pin, then do the same from the other corner, leaving you with a triangle for the base and two remnants for another project. Repeat with the other square to make the lid. As neatly as you can, finish the raw edges of the triangles. It is slightly harder to zig-zag along these sorts of edges, but take it slow and steady and it will look fine.

4 Hand stitch the bottom of the box to the sides all the way around, but stitch the lid only along one side to form a hinge. Trim as desired.

Top tip

It is too fiddly to cut a triangle of rug canvas and
then try to weave and stitch it, believe me!

Cylindrical box

This box requires three pieces of rug canvas: one rectangle for the box and two circles for the base and lid. Geometry class was a long time ago, so I always wait until I have woven, stitched, and backed the main part of the box and sewn the edges together before making a quick paper pattern for the circle base and lid.

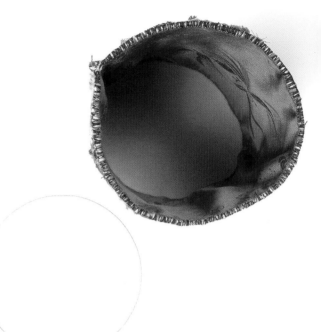

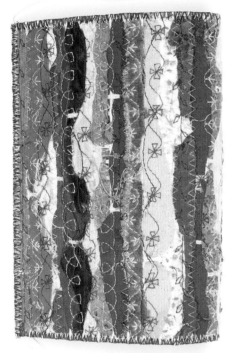

1 The body of the box is simply one piece of Rug canvas fabric that you back in the usual way (see page 28). Machine stitch a vertical seam to create the cylinder shape and roll it between your hands to make it as round as you can, like a tube.

2 Stand the cylinder on a piece of paper and draw around the end to make a paper pattern for the base and lid. Weave two squares that are a little larger than you think you will need for these pieces.

3 Place the paper pattern on the first square and cut out your base, then repeat for the lid.

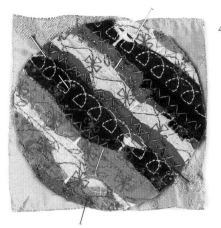

4 Pin the cut-out circles of Rug canvas fabric to the lining,

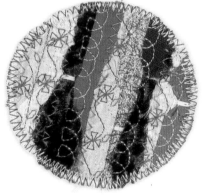

5 Stitch around twice before trimming the backing fabric and then finish off with as many rows of zig-zag stitching as you feel is necessasry. Rug canvas fabric that is not cut right along the lines of canvas thread can be tricky to finish off, so go slowly and carefully.

6 Hand stitch the base to the bottom of the box. I like to leave round lids loose so they can be removed completely, and to aid this lid's removal I've attached a Sweet bead (page 30). (A finished example of this box is shown top right on page 52.)

Decorative details

You've probably noticed that I've decorated a lot of the boxes in this book with Sweet beads. But I wouldn't want you to think that you are limited to this option, so think about how you could use a Fabric Flower (page 78) or a Nail-polish button (page 41). And I'm sure you could think of something to do with a length of machine-wrap cord (page 36).

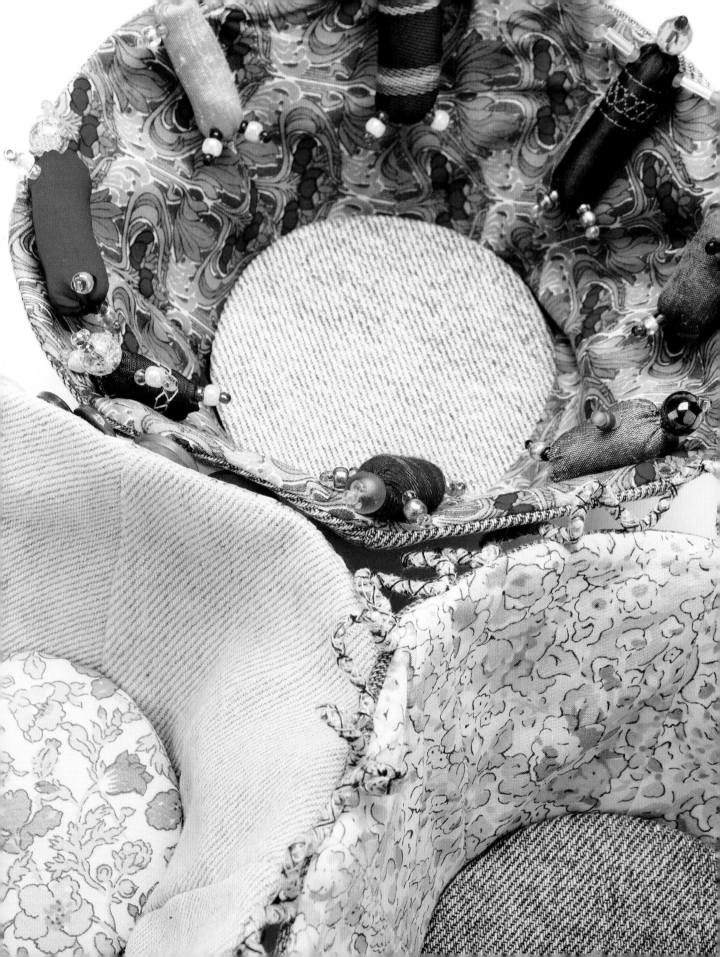

Fabric Bowls

I've been the height I am now since I was 13, which meant that I needed to learn to sew quick or live with trousers that were too short or shirts that were too grown up! Darts used to drive me mad, but I've since found them terribly useful when designing these Fabric Bowls.

I love using wildly contrasting fabrics for these bowls. Delicate Liberty Tana Lawn and well-worn denim from recycled jeans are my favourites.

These bowls have many uses: holding office supplies on my desk, cotton-wool balls in the bathroom, sweets in the living room, and for odds and ends on my dressing table.

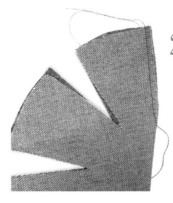

2 With the right sides together, start stitching the darts.

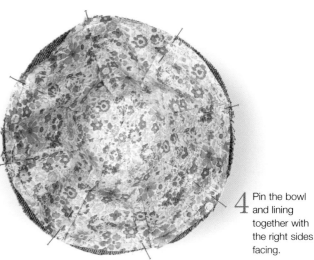

3 Once all eight darts on the bowl are stitched, repeat for the lining.

1 Cut a bowl and a lining using the template on page 94.

4 Pin the bowl and lining together with the right sides facing.

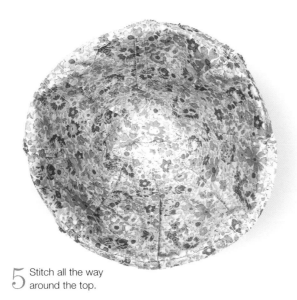

5 Stitch all the way around the top.

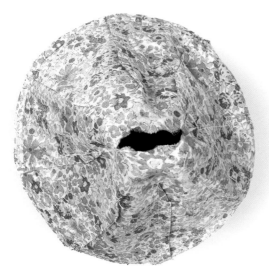

6 Pull the fabrics apart a little and cut a 2.5–4cm (1–1⅛in) slit through the lining fabric (this will be hidden by the base). Turn the bowl right side out through that cut. Lightly press all around the top edge.

Top tip

If you are going to decorate the fabric you have chosen in some way (such as machine-couching, page 34), make sure to cut a circle slightly larger to allow for any shrinkage caused by lines of stitches.

To make the base

Cut a bowl base out of fabric and a slightly smaller insert for the base out of card (not any lighter weight than say a cereal box, though) using the patterns on page 95. If you happen to have some scraps of wadding (batting), you can cut a piece the same size as the card, but this isn't strictly necessary.

1 Lay the base fabric right side down, add the wadding (if using it) and then the card.

2 Run a gathering stitch all the way around the edge of the base fabric by hand. Pull up the gathering stitches and tie tightly. Place in the bottom of the bowl.

Decorating the bowls

For trims around the edges of bowls, try using Sweet beads (page 30), Nail-polish buttons (page 41), "No-worries" Dolls (page 86), or a length of machine-wrap cord (page 36). Button blooms (page 40) could also look good. Of course, you can add anything else that you think would be the perfect decoration.

Rolled-fabric beads

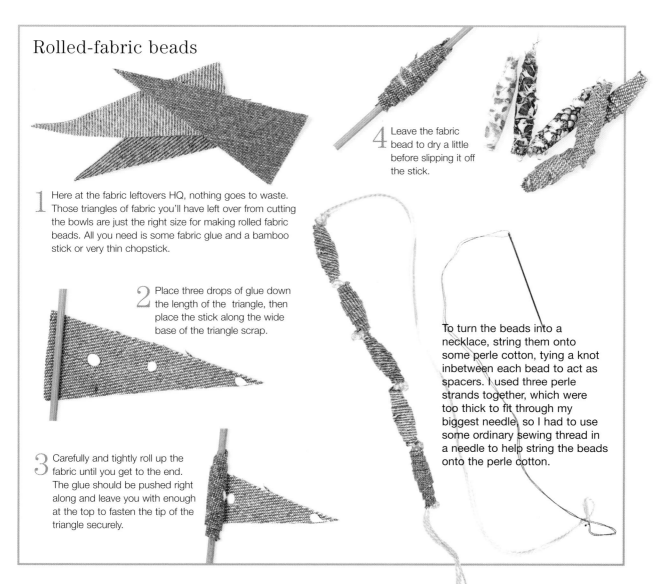

1 Here at the fabric leftovers HQ, nothing goes to waste. Those triangles of fabric you'll have left over from cutting the bowls are just the right size for making rolled fabric beads. All you need is some fabric glue and a bamboo stick or very thin chopstick.

2 Place three drops of glue down the length of the triangle, then place the stick along the wide base of the triangle scrap.

3 Carefully and tightly roll up the fabric until you get to the end. The glue should be pushed right along and leave you with enough at the top to fasten the tip of the triangle securely.

4 Leave the fabric bead to dry a little before slipping it off the stick.

To turn the beads into a necklace, string them onto some perle cotton, tying a knot inbetween each bead to act as spacers. I used three perle strands together, which were too thick to fit through my biggest needle, so I had to use some ordinary sewing thread in a needle to help string the beads onto the perle cotton.

One-piece Clutch Bag

■ Technique used: Rug canvas fabric (page 24)

This one-piece evening bag is very closely related to the frames on page 72 and is made out of Rug canvas fabric. You can make a tiny evening bag or something more substantial – it's entirely up to you. I would advise leaving a minimum of four rows across the top for the handle and making the hole for the handle big enough so that your knuckles don't rub up against the bag when you hold it. You want to be able to hold it comfortably!

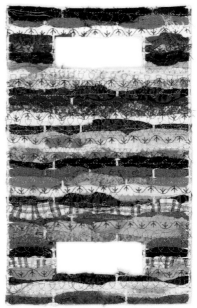

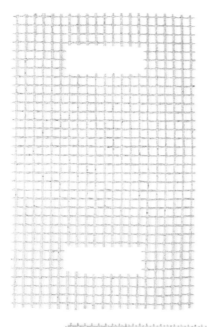

1 All you really need to do before weaving and stitching is to make sure that the holes you have cut for handles match up evenly when you fold the bag in half. Honestly, that's it.

2 So, weave, stitch, and back the bag as you would for the frame. And, if you feel the urge, add some machine-couching (page 34).

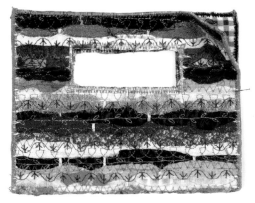

3 Fold the bag in half, right sides together, and stitch from the bottom edge of the bag ONLY to the bottom edge of the handle.

4 A good strong popper (snap) sewn to the lining just below the handle is all you need to keep the bag closed. Use whatever sort of trim you desire to finish off your bag.

Design your bag size to fit exactly (or only) what you need.

Top tip

If you want quite a large bag, you can always make one in two pieces first (see Flat Cases, page 76) and then sew them together after weaving, stitching, and backing the two separate pieces.

Leftover Fabric Bag

If you have a rectangle of fabric you can make this pattern-less bag. There's a basic lined version with matching fabric handles, plus two variations.

I used a piece of fabric 38 x 23cm (15 x 9in), which made a bag 15cm (6in) tall by 19cm (7½in) wide by 8cm (3in) deep, but you can scale the measurements up or down as you please, with 2.5cm (1in) in either direction making no odds.

2 Fold the fabric in half horizontally, right sides together, and put a pin in the fold at the bottom.

3 Stitch up one of the side edges.

4 Line up the seam you just stitched with the pin at the bottom of the bag. Pin and sew across.

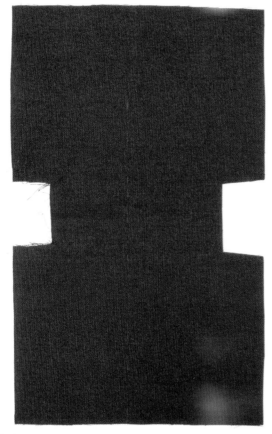

1 Cut out two rectangles 4cm (1½in) wide by 7cm (2¾in) high along the long edges, centred over the horizontal middle line of the bag. Now you can use this piece of fabric as a template for cutting a lining for the bag (saves measuring everything twice!). You could choose a patterned lining, as I have, or go for a contrasting solid colour.

5 Repeat steps 3 and 4 on the other side, and you have a basic bag!

6 Assemble the lining in the same way, but leave an opening of around 5cm (2in) along one of the side seams.

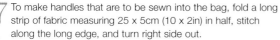

7 To make handles that are to be sewn into the bag, fold a long strip of fabric measuring 25 x 5cm (10 x 2in) in half, stitch along the long edge, and turn right side out.

Top tip

If you are going to use something like the nice thick cord of a quality shop's carrier bag, wait until you assemble the bag with its lining before attaching this type of handle.

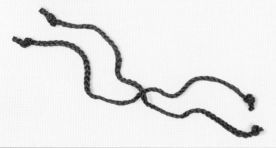

8 Pin the handles to the outside of the bag and baste along the upper edge to hold them in place.

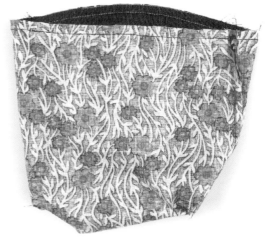

9 Place the lining inside the bag with the right sides facing, covering the handles. Pin the upper edge and machine stitch all the way around. Turn the bag through the gap in the lining and slipstitch to close. Turn the bag right side out.

10 If you are using cord for handles simply stitch them on, now that all the machine sewing is complete.

Using LCP to make a deeper bag

■ Techniques used: Lazy crazy patchwork, Machine-couching, and Machine-wrap cord, (pages 22, 34, and 36)

I added strips of LCP to the short edges to create a deeper bag. Then I jazzed up the rather plain handles, which I sewed between the bag and the lining (step 9, previous page), by machine-couching some orange and pink machine-wrap cord onto them.

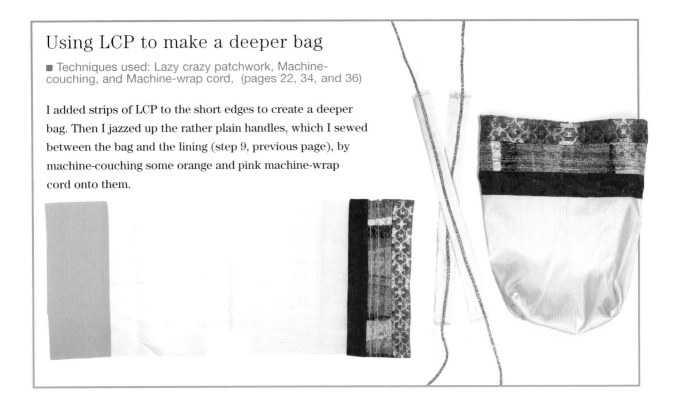

Using LCP to make a wider bag

■ Technique used: Lazy crazy patchwork (page 22)

I made a wider bag by cutting the fabric straight down the vertical centre and inserting a 5cm (2in) strip of LCP. I made up the bag in the same way, adding a nice silk lining and some machine-embroidered green handles.

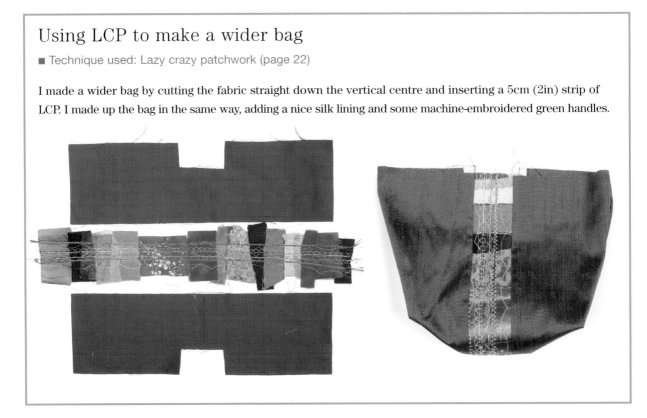

Top tips

Strips of Ruched fabric (see page 39) also make terrific handles. For ideas on how to add a little extra something to your bag, check out the various Fabric Flowers (see page 78).

Photograph Frames

■ Technique used: Rug canvas fabric (page 24)

You have so many choices for a Rug canvas fabric photo frame design that you might spend more time thinking about the frames than actually making them. What size do you want? Would you like more than one opening for pictures? Would you like it trimmed? Do you want to hang it on a wall or stand it on a desk? Once your mind is made up, you can get started!

If you have a specific photo in mind, use that to determine the size of the frame and the opening you will need. The following steps show you how to make a double frame that can stand up on its own (or be left unstiffened to hang on a wall), but if you would rather make a miniature frame with a magnet for your fridge, a large single frame, or even a long thin one for a great landscape shot, go right ahead. The basics are pretty much the same.

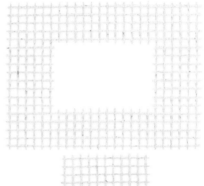

1 The first step is to decide on the size of your frame. Looking at the examples above, your frame could have two different-sized openings, or both could be traditional landscape shapes or even small squares. Be sure to allow at least three rows of squares around the edge and inbetween the two openings. This is for strength and also to create a sufficiently large surface area for stitching.

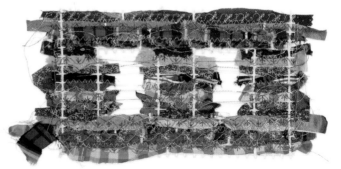

2 Decide whether you want your rows of colour to run vertically or horizontally across the finished frame, then weave your fabric. Now just stitch right across from one end to the other, ignoring the openings you have cut for your photographs.

3 Trim away all the excess thread and fabric from the outside of the frame and also the openings for the photographs. Then choose an attractive backing fabric.

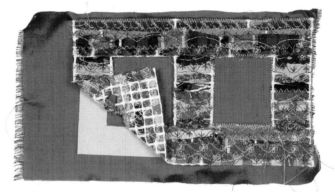

4 Cut an insert from card slightly smaller than the trimmed frame and sandwich it in between the frame and lining. (Alternatively, just place the lining and frame together for the hanging version.) Zig-zag once around the outside edges, then around the openings. Trim again, more closely than the first time.

5 Continue stitching, using as many rows of zig-zag as you like, then hand stitch pieces of ribbon in an "X" across the back of the frames in order to hold your photos in place.

Fabric photo pocket

Another option for holding your photo in place is to cut a piece of fabric larger than the space for the photo, finish the edge in whatever way you wish (plain or decorative stitching), and stitch this to the back of the frame, leaving the upper edge free to insert your photo. This is a good idea for a larger frame, where the photo might be too heavy for ribbons to hold it in place.

To hang the frame

Small frames can have a magnet glued to the back. Larger frames can have a decorative loop at the top, or you can conceal a hook at the back. Three or more small frames can be attached in a line to a strip of ribbon or fabric, which can then be decorated.

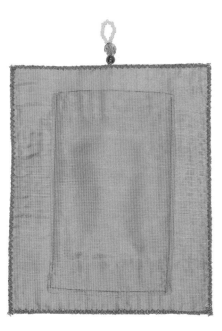

Top tips

An assortment of Sweet beads (page 30), Rug canvas fabric shapes (page 91) and even Button blooms (page 40) gives the selection of frames on page 72 a little extra dash. Think about using machine-wrap cord (page 36) and even some tiny Fabric Flowers (starting from page 78). But remember, the more you add the more you'll need to make sure you've made a good sturdy loop from which to hang your frame!

Wallets and cases

■ Technique used: Rug canvas fabric (page 24)

You can use Rug canvas fabric for all sorts of things, not just the projects I have walked you through in this book. All you need to do, as I have done here with the sunglasses case, is make sure that whatever you weave and stitch is large enough for your item, which involves leaving a few extra rug canvas holes around the edge. The sunglasses and CD cases both comprise two identical pieces of RCF, which, once you have backed them, are stitched together on three sides with the basic method (page 53).

Fold-over cases

These cases can be just about any size you like and used for just about anything you want, and the beauty of them is that you can't go wrong – they always work! To calculate the size, decide on how wide you want it to be, and how long, then take the length measurement and multiply it by two and a half. These two measurements give you the size to which you need to cut your rug canvas.

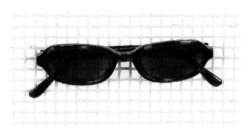

Leave a little room around the edges.

Cases for CDs and sunglasses

1 Weave, stitch, and back your piece. Cut a piece of sew-on touch-and-close fastening a little bit narrower than the strip you've made. Sew the fuzzy side to one end of the RCF strip, right side up.

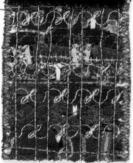

2 Now flip the strip over to the lining side and sew the plastic loopy side of the touch-and-close to the opposite end.

3 Fold up the case to the height desired, and stitch the side edges.

This case is now ready for use as a mobile (cell) phone holder. Variations on the same technique (shown above) can be used as an evening bag, coin purse, and credit-card holder.

Top tip

You can use stick-on touch-and-close fastening too, but I would sew it on anyway just to be sure it stays in place.

Fabric Flowers

As you will see over the next four pages, I couldn't decide on just one "scrap" flower for the book, so I've chosen Folded Flowers, Stacked Flowers, Loopy Flowers, and Ruched Flowers. I'm sure you'll think of dozens of different ways to use them.

Folded flowers

This project is great for those of you who have tubs of leftover precisely cut squares. However, if you're cutting them just for this project, don't worry: they needn't be rotary-cut precise. Don't even make a paper pattern or draw perfect squares on the back of the fabric: just cut and fold.

1 Cut some squares from your chosen fabric. You'll need five to make one flower.

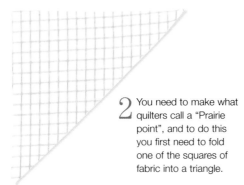

2 You need to make what quilters call a "Prairie point", and to do this you first need to fold one of the squares of fabric into a triangle.

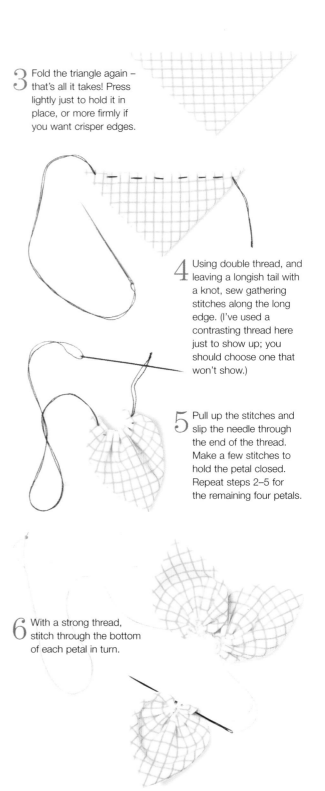

3 Fold the triangle again – that's all it takes! Press lightly just to hold it in place, or more firmly if you want crisper edges.

4 Using double thread, and leaving a longish tail with a knot, sew gathering stitches along the long edge. (I've used a contrasting thread here just to show up; you should choose one that won't show.)

5 Pull up the stitches and slip the needle through the end of the thread. Make a few stitches to hold the petal closed. Repeat steps 2–5 for the remaining four petals.

6 With a strong thread, stitch through the bottom of each petal in turn.

7 Once all five petals are on the thread, close the loop as in step 5, then stitch through the first petal again.

Folded flower bouquet

The button centre is first twisted onto the end of some green florist wire and then has a few drops of glue applied to its back. Once slid through the centre of a folded flower, it can be left to dry.

Top tip

There certainly is no good reason to have all matching fabric in a flower! Why not layer contrasting flowers to make a "double bloom" or make each petal from a different fabric.

A large spool of thread "vase" is just right for these lovely Liberty Tana Lawn flowers.

Stacked Flowers

On page 95 you'll find three templates for this six-petal flower. I've used one of each size here, but if you want to make fuller, fatter flowers, use more than one of each of the three sizes.

1 Depending on the thickness of the fabric and the fullness you want for your flower, cut at least one of each size petal.

3 Stack the flower pieces so that the stitched segments cross each other at different angles. Choose some centres, maybe beads, ribbon rosebuds, or Sweet beads (page 30).

2 To give each flower section a little shape, fold roughly in half with the right sides together and zig-zag stitch a part of the middle.

4 Secure together with strong thread and attach the centres. I've used a Nail-polish button (page 40), a cluster of sequins, and a decorative flower from some gift packaging.

Loopy Flowers

■ Technique used: Machine-wrap cord (page 36)

To make an airy, open flower you will need about 1.2m (4ft) of machine-wrap cord.

Loop the cord around your thumb and stitch with doubled thread through both bits of the cord to hold the first petal. Slide the loop off your thumb and make the next one (being sure to butt it right up against the first).

After several petals, you'll find the cord coils around itself to form the base of the flower. Keep going until you get to about 2.5cm (1in) from the end, then push the tail down through the centre of the spiralled flower to the back.

Ruched Flowers

■ Technique used: Ruched fabric (page 39)

These soft flowers with their crumpled petals can be the perfect decoration for many projects. To give you an idea of size: 9cm (3½in) strip of finished Ruched fabric gives a flower just 4cm (1½in) wide.

1 Using a strip of ruched fabric, curl one end into a circle and hold it together at the back with a few stitches.

2 Continue wrapping around in a circle, holding the edges together as needed with a stitch or two.

3 Once you reach the end of the fabric, fasten off securely.

"No-cal Candy"

A small silk sample book came my way and I took it apart at once, not wanting the staples to rust into the fabric. I was going to sort them by colour, since they were all the same shape and fabric content, but ended up putting the whole lot in a little plastic tub of their own. However, one piece escaped to the floor, got a little crumpled up, and was mistaken for a sweetie paper. In an instant, a use was found for all 36 bits of silk!

4 Pull up and fasten off. Stitch the other end in the same way, but before pulling up the stitches pack firmly with toy filling or cotton-wool balls. If you want to add some decoration, seed beads are the ideal size.

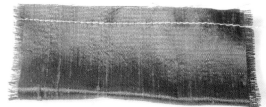

1 Fold the fabric right sides together and sew with a short-length stitch.

2 Turn right side out and fray the edges a little (or use pinking shears for a different decorative effect).

3 Run a gathering stitch all the way around one end, about one-fifth of the way in from the edge.

Christmas-tree garland

A garland of these looks great on a Christmas tree. When making the garland, you need to create your candies around the cord or ribbon, so slip the tubes on before you stitch and stuff the candy.

Jujus

■ Technique used: Rug canvas fabric (page 24)

Hollywood has a lot to answer for when it comes to voodoo. True practitioners see it as channelling the forces of nature for positive means, whereas what we often see in movies is much more sinister and negative. All those pins! A juju is a totem, a talisman, a poppet, which, when carried about your person in a certain way, channels these positive energies of the earth. You can put one under your pillow to improve communication, carry one in your pocket for wealth and prosperity, hang one from your belt for fertility, and wear one close to your heart for love. If one doesn't work for you in the way you hoped, pass it on to someone else.

2 Secure a long piece of thread to the square bit of RCF (the body), and add a bead for the head. Place as much thread hair over the thread as you want. If you fancy giving your juju a hat rather than (or as well as) some hair, try a button or large sequin.

1 Start with a little scrap of Rug canvas fabric, backed in the usual way (see page 28). Consider how you want to form your juju's limbs, head, and hair. I used mostly beads on this juju, but you could also use wire, buttons, or whatever else you have to hand to "flesh out" the limbs. As for the hair, I chose to use some of the "thread vermicelli" I talked about on page 13, but you could dream up your own crafty ideas.

3 Loop the fastening thread around the hair and go back down through the head bead. Secure the thread at the neck then run it through the top edge of the RCF to the first arm spot.

4 Create the arm in much the same way as you would for the dangles on Tassels (page 88).

5 Run the thread through the edge of the RCF to come out at the other arm spot. Complete the arm, then form the legs in the same way. (If you want to attach each limb with a separate thread, that's just fine.)

6 Glue a small pin back on when you are done. Or use a magnet so that your little juju can live on your fridge at home, or filing cabinet at work.

Top tip

If you want to wear your juju as a brooch, insert a scatter pin finding through the lining *before* you stitch it to the bit of RCF at the start of the project, then attach it to your lapel with the matching clutch.

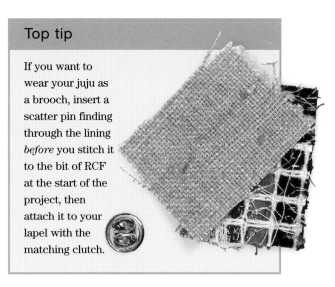

Sweet bead jujus

■ Technique used: Sweet beads (page 30)

You could make a tube as you would for a Sweet bead, but sew the ends flat instead of gathering them, and use that for the body. You can also vary the size and your short jujus can hang around with their slimmer RCF cousins.

"No-worries" dolls

■ Technique used: Sweet beads (page 30)

You may have heard of Guatemalan worry dolls (You whisper your troubles to them and they magically take them away.) Well, mine are (country of your choice) "No-worries" dolls: fat, happy, and content with their lot in life. Tell THEM your troubles and they'll remind you that you live in a country with electricity, running water, freedom of speech, and chocolate, and gently urge you to go for a walk, read a book, give blood, or play with a puppy.

It's best to use the same thread for the head and all of the little limbs; a doubled-up piece measuring 35cm (14in) should be fine. Since these little Sweet bead figures are rather small, I don't clutter them up with mismatched arms and legs as I do for the jujus (page 84) – I just find a nice head bead and go to my box of seed and other tiny matching beads for the limbs.

2 After fastening the head bead, make sure your needle comes out of the Sweet bead right where you want to place the first arm.

3 Thread on three small beads.

1 Such a little thing needs only a single bead for the head, but you'll also have to use a tiny seed bead as a stopper to keep it from falling off the Sweet bead body!

4 Pass the needle back through the beads, skipping the last one that was threaded.

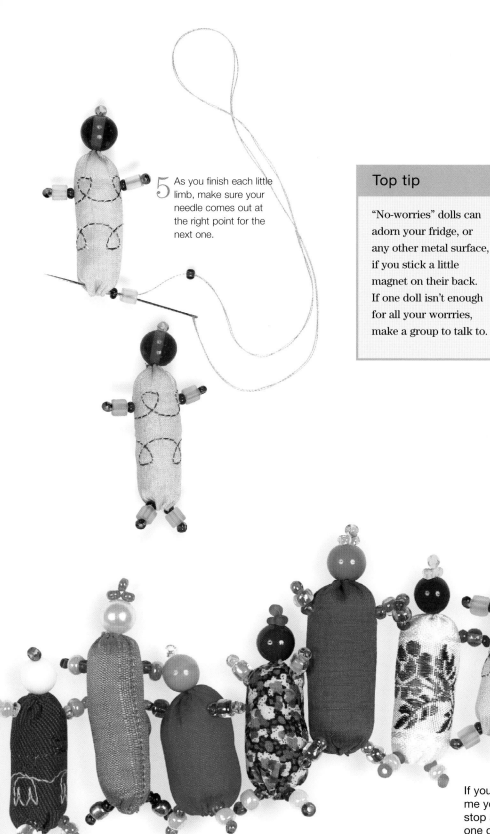

5 As you finish each little limb, make sure your needle comes out at the right point for the next one.

Top tip

"No-worries" dolls can adorn your fridge, or any other metal surface, if you stick a little magnet on their back. If one doll isn't enough for all your worrries, make a group to talk to.

If you are anything like me you won't be able to stop after making just one doll.

Tassels

■ Technique used: Sweet beads (page 30)

Sweet beads of all sizes lend themselves to simple tassel-making. Attach them to the ends of plain scarves, or dress up a little drawstring bag.

You can use Sweet beads made of any fabric, and if you've found that some have turned out a little large to use for the tiny "No-worries" dolls (page 86), why not use them for a tassel head instead? If you are going to use heavier wools or velvets, you need to start with a larger scrap than usual to account for the thickness created in the seam allowance (both the machine-stitched edge and the two edges that get turned under when you stitch and stuff).

2 Take the needle down through the last large bead you added before the seed beads.

1 Thread on as many beads as you like for the top, then add about ten small seed beads for the loop. If you need a bigger loop at the top, add fifteen, twenty, or however many fit the bill.

3 Continue into the tassel head and make a few stitches back and forth at the top for strength' before finishing off the thread and bringing it down to the bottom of the tassel head to start the dangles.

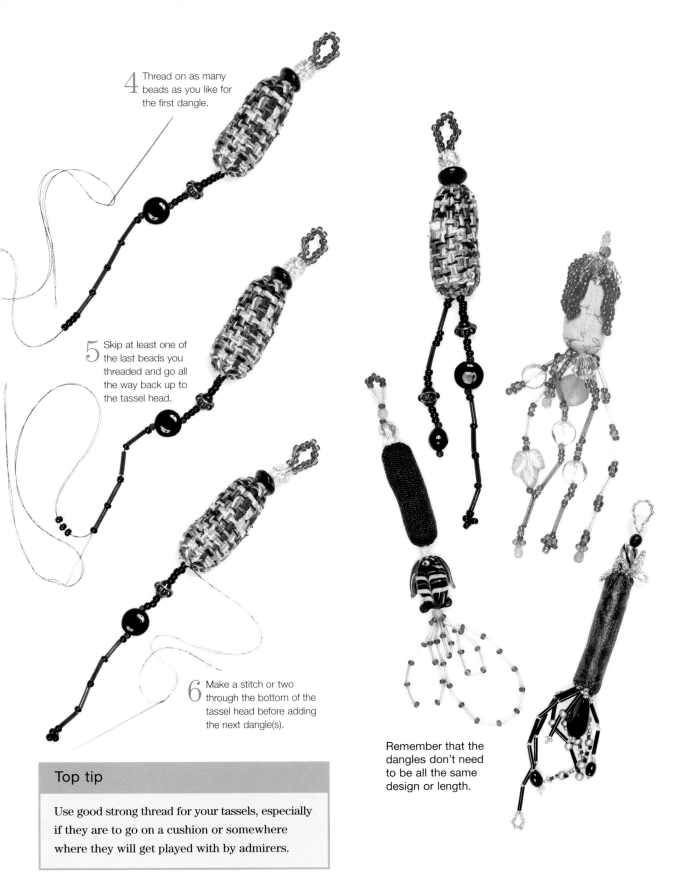

4 Thread on as many beads as you like for the first dangle.

5 Skip at least one of the last beads you threaded and go all the way back up to the tassel head.

6 Make a stitch or two through the bottom of the tassel head before adding the next dangle(s).

Top tip

Use good strong thread for your tassels, especially if they are to go on a cushion or somewhere where they will get played with by admirers.

Remember that the dangles don't need to be all the same design or length.

Jewellery

■ Techniques used: Rug canvas fabric, Sweet beads, and Machine-couching (pages 24, 30, and 34)

We are near the end of the book now and I am running out of space for all my ideas for using up those leftover fabric scraps, so I'll just pass on a few ideas about how to turn some of the things you've already made into jewellery.

Sweet-bead earrings are quick to make (and deceptively light on the earlobe), as are the hat pins shown here. Thread a bead or two onto a hat pin, then pierce a Sweet bead through the middle. Add a tiny drop of glue to the bottom of the Sweet bead, and push a final bead on to hold it together.

Tiny scraps of Rug canvas fabric also make attractive earrings. Decorate them with a few bugle beads or machine-couch some metallic cord in place, before adding a jump ring and ear wire to finish them.

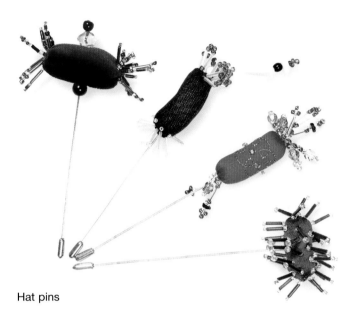

Hat pins

Jewellery shapes

■ Technique used: Rug canvas fabric (page 24)

Scraps of Rug canvas fabric left over from bigger projects, or little pieces you make up as samples, can be used for all sorts of jewellery. Simply back the fabric pieces using the method on page 28, and then adapt them as you wish: turn them into earrings, string them onto necklaces or bracelets ... the choice is yours. And don't think you have to stick to regular square-shaped pieces, such as those used for Boxes – just look above for some very successful jewellery shapes. But do remember that curved edges can be a little trickier to zig-zag along, so take your time.

Top tips

A strip of Rug canvas fabric can become a stylish cuff quite easily. It's just a narrow version of the fold-over purse on page 76, so follow those directions for attaching a touch-and-close closure on each end of a piece of RCF, this time cut to fit your wrist. Trim with Sweet beads for a funky charm bracelet, or maybe use a strip to replace your old watch strap. Or, make some tiny versions of the Fabric Flowers starting on page 78 and stitch those to it.

You could also make a cool bracelet out of the machine-wrap cord and bead method I talk about on page 38, using the fastening method on page 92.

Machine-wrap cord and Sweet beads were made for each other in the necklace department. You can add a stitch to hold the beads apart or let them all bunch together. Or, more simply, a single Sweet bead on a length of ribbon or chain can be rather effective.

Choosing fabrics for jewellery gives you the ideal opportunity to create that perfect outfit. Pick colours that complement a new dress or jacket to make the ultimate co-ordinated look. You can also keep reminders of past favourites that you either grew out of or grew tired of: use some fabric scraps to make shapes for necklaces or earrings, and enjoy that old blouse or skirt all over again – just in miniature.

A final thought, before I leave you with the neat necklace-fastening idea below: why not make a large RCF box (page 52) in which to store all your wonderful new jewellery? It seems only right!

Necklace fastener

■ Techniques used: Rug canvas fabric and Machine-wrap cord (pages 24 and 36)

A very easy necklace fastener for a Rug canvas fabric and Machine-wrap cord necklace is the humble popper (snap fastener). With such a large chunky heart (nearly 8cm/3in across), I thought one "strand" of cord would be too thin, so I made a piece three times as long as I needed and tripled it up. Using some strong thread, I whip-stitched the edges together and added the popper halves. I then stitched one end to the back of the brown RCF heart. This is very easy to put around your neck, because you don't have to fiddle blindly with small catches behind your head!

Templates

Fabric Bowl template (page 63)

PLACE ON FOLD

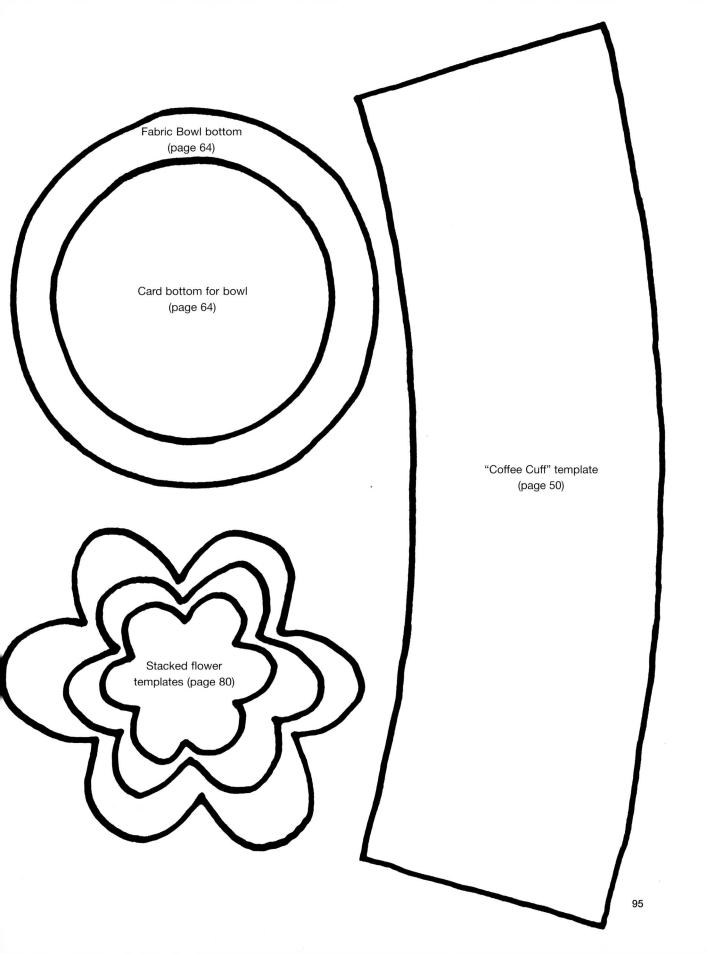

Fabric Bowl bottom
(page 64)

Card bottom for bowl
(page 64)

"Coffee Cuff" template
(page 50)

Stacked flower
templates (page 80)

Index

Acknowledgments

Nancy for setting me on the crafting path, Alice for hiring me for Liberty's Sewing School, Linden for being enthusiastic (especially when I wasn't), and Anna and Alison for teaching me everything I need to know about writing my first (of many!) books.